PERFECT PHRASES in

Italian

for Confident Travel

**The No *Faux-Pas* Phrasebook
for the Perfect Trip**

Salvatore Bancheri and Michael Lettieri

New York   Chicago   San Francisco   Lisbon   London   Madrid   Mexico City
Milan   New Delhi   San Juan   Seoul   Singapore   Sydney   Toronto

Library of Congress Cataloging-in-Publication Data

Bancheri, Salvatore, 1954–
    Perfect phrases in Italian for confident travel / Salvatore Bancheri
and Michael Lettieri.
        p.   cm.— (Perfect phrases)
    Text in English and Italian
    ISBN 0-07-150824-4 (alk. paper)
    1. Italian language—Conversation and phrase books—English.
    I. Lettieri, Michael.   II. Title.

    PC1121 B36   2009
    458.2'421—dc22   2008052330

1 2 3 4 5 6 7 8 9 10 11 12 13 14 15 16 17 18 19 20 FGR/FGR 0 9

ISBN   978-0-07-150824-7
MHID   0-07-150824-4

McGraw-Hill books are available at special quantity discounts to use as
premiums and sales promotions or for use in corporate training programs.
To contact a representative, please visit the Contact Us pages at
www.mhprofessional.com.

This book is printed on acid-free paper.

Contents

Contents

Introduction

Did you know that Italians don't leave tips at restaurants? Or that Italians do not order cappuccinos after breakfast? When visiting Italy, a faux pas like tipping at a restaurant or ordering a cappuccino at lunchtime wouldn't create much of a problem. In the first case, the waiter will appreciate your generosity; in the second case, he or she will probably just smile and recognize you as a tourist. Unfortunately, a cultural faux pas in a different situation could cause you a good deal of embarrassment or even offend your companions. When traveling to Italy, or to any other country for that matter, cultural awareness is fundamental to enjoying a perfect trip.

Italians love when a tourist tries to speak their language. They'll appreciate your effort even if they hear their language spoken with an imperfect pronunciation. They'll even go out of their way to help you if you request information, directions, or advice in their language. However, your Italian might not be as effective if your request is not culturally appropriate. Nonverbal communication and cultural awareness will open the door to understanding and enjoying Italian culture and people.

Perfect Phrases in Italian for Confident Travel will give you the fundamental tools you need to communicate effectively, speak with confidence, and avoid cultural embarrassment. Each chapter is based on the most common situations a traveler might encounter. The topics include dining out, driving, and many other everyday activities. Each chapter contains high-frequency sentences and expressions designed to make your visit to Italy easier and more enjoyable, but, more importantly, each main phrase is followed by detailed cultural insights explaining its context. These entries are then followed by extra phrases that will greatly improve your ability to communicate and converse. Each of these phrases is accompanied by an English translation and a phonetic transcription that approximates the Italian pronunciation using common English sounds. This pragmatic approach will help you achieve the most effective level of communication using the least amount of language, all in a culturally sound context.

The cultural insights offered in this book will give you a better understanding and deeper appreciation of Italian life and culture. The everyday phrases will help you communicate effectively to make your trip even more memorable.

Buon viaggio!   Have a great trip!
Boo-ON vee-AD-jee-oh

Pronunciation Guide

Each Italian phrase in this book is accompanied by an English translation and a phonetic transcription that approximates the Italian pronunciation using common English sounds. Both components should help make you a more confident speaker of Italian. The phonetic transcriptions are broken down by syllables, with the stressed syllable capitalized. Keep in mind that most Italian words are stressed on the second-to-last syllable, but there are exceptions. Here you will find a brief explanation of Italian sounds, particularly those that present some difficulties to English speakers.

Vowels

When pronouncing Italian words, please remember that all vowels must be pronounced clearly—this is the key to being understood by native speakers. Unlike English, Italian vowels always have the same sound, no matter their position in a word:

- **A** is always pronounced like the *a* in *father, party*
- **E** is always pronounced like the *e* in *met, get*
- **I** is always pronounced like the *i* in *police, machine*
- **O** is always pronounced like the *o* in *cold, gold*
- **U** is always pronounced like the *oo* in *moon, soon*

Consonants

The sounds of most consonants (**b**, **d**, **f**, **g**, **l**, **m**, **n**, **p**, **q**, **r**, **s**, **t**, **v**, **z**) in Italian are very similar to those in English. Pronounce them as you would in English and you will be easily understood.

The letter **h** at the beginning of a word is always silent. When it appears after **c** or **g**, however, it gives those letters a "hard" sound.

The **c** and **g** in Italian have two different sounds, depending on the letter that follows them in a word. They have a soft sound (like the *ch* in *church* or the *g* in *gem*) when followed by the vowels **e** or **i**: **cena**, **cinema, gelato, gioco**. They have a hard sound (as in *cat* or *go*) when followed by the vowels **a**, **o**, **u**, or the letter **h**: **casa**, **gatto**, **cono**, **gusto**, **funghi**, **chiesa**.

Letter Combinations

The combination **gn** does not exist in English; it is approximately equivalent to the *ni* in *onion*. The transcriptions in this book represent this sound by using *ny*.

Gli is roughly equivalent to the *li* in *million*. If **gl** is followed by any other vowel, it is pronounced as in English.

It is important to pronounce double consonants, since words like **casa** and **cassa** can have vastly different meanings (in this case, *house* and *case*, respectively). When you have a double consonant you need to prolong the sound and then shorten the vowel that follows.

These few points, when combined with the intuitive phonetic transcriptions in the book, should help you acquire an easily comprehensible pronunciation. Don't worry about having a slightly foreign accent when traveling in Italy. It will charm the Italians you speak to, and it might even give you an aura of sophistication.

Chapter 1

Greetings and Introductions

 Buongiorno. Come sta? *(Boo-on-JOR-no CO-meh stah):*
Good morning. How are you?

In Italian there are two different ways of addressing people: formally and informally. To address someone formally, use the *Lei* form; to address someone informally, use the *tu* form. So, for example, the simple question "How are you?" has two possible translations: the formal *Come sta (Lei)?*, and the informal *Come stai (tu)?* The *Lei* form is required with almost every person over age sixteen, unless you are speaking to a family member or a close friend. Using *Lei* is a form of respect, but sometimes it may create a certain distance between speakers. On the other hand, some people may be offended when addressed in the *tu* form. To be on the safe side, start by addressing everyone with the *Lei* form until the person you are talking to says: *Diamoci del tu* (let's use the *tu* form), which gives you permission to use the familiar form.

Students are required to use the *Lei* form with all their teachers/ professors, at all levels. After grade five, teachers start to address students in the polite form as well. When calling out names, teachers use a student's last name, not first name. Even among work colleagues, it is common to use the *Lei* form.

Italians often say that even they have trouble with the use of *tu* and *Lei/voi*. Usually, but not always, they use *tu* with someone with whom they're on a first-name basis. In certain parts of Italy, and especially in the south, the *Lei* form is sometimes replaced by the *voi* form when addressing a person formally. So, "How are you, Mr. Smith?" can be translated as *Come state (voi), Signor Smith?* The *voi* form has a degree of formality that is even greater than *Lei*. The question of formality is actually easier if you're not Italian, because you can just use *Lei* with everyone over sixteen until you're told to say *tu*.

Come sta, signor Carli?   How are you, Mr. Carli?
CO-meh stah seen-YOR CAHR-lee
Come stai, amico mio?   How are you, my friend?
CO-meh STAH-ee ah-MEE-coh
     MEE-oh

 Dottor Risi, buongiorno. *(dot-TOR REE-zee boo-on-JOR-no):* Dr. Risi, good morning.

Italians love to be addressed by their titles. Although in America we rarely use titles before last names (preferring instead to use the simple *Mr./Mrs./Miss*), Italians always use the title of their profession before their last name. Some of the most common titles are: *avvocato, ingegnere, dottore, professore, ragioniere*, etc. So, to address Mr. Smith who is a lawyer, one would say: *Buongiorno, avvocato (Smith)*. Remember that in Italy, a university degree entitles the holder to be called *dottore*. Furthermore, certain high school diplomas (*ragioniere, geometra, perito agrario*) will be enough to guarantee someone a title.

Most titles also have equivalent female forms; for example, a female doctor is a *dottoressa* and a female professor is a *professoressa*. However, for professions which were once male dominated, like *avvocato*, *ingegnere*, *ministro*, *presidente*, etc., the tendency today is to use the male title for women as well. For example, if Mrs. Rossi is a lawyer or a doctor, one could say: *Buongiorno, avvocato Rossi!* or *Buongiorno, dottor Rossi!*, omitting the use of the feminine form of the title. For titles that end in an *e*, the final *e* is dropped before the last name: *l'ingegner Bianchi*, whether male or female.

Arrivederla, Professoressa Binni.   Good-bye, Professor Binni.
Ar-ree-veh-DAIR-lah pro-fes-
    so-RES-sah BEEN-nee
Ecco l'avvocato Maria Lima.   Here is the lawyer Maria Lima.
EC-co lahv-vo-CAH-toh Mah-REE-ah
    LI-mah

 Buongiorno, signora! *(Boo-on-JOR-no seen-YO-rah):* Good morning, ma'am!

Buongiorno, or *buon giorno*, is one of the most common forms of salutation in Italy. It can be used both formally and informally with strangers or with friends, while entering a coffee shop, in a doctor's office, or while walking in the streets. For example, Italian shopkeepers expect shoppers to say *Buongiorno* upon entering their shop. As with 'morning in English, the salutation can sometimes be shortened to simply *'giorno* or *'ngiorno*, followed by a nod. Other times, it is necessary to add a title to the salutation: *Buongiorno, professore* (Good morning, Professor), *Buongiorno, dottore* (Good morning, Doctor), *Buongiorno, signora* (Good morning, Ma'am). You seldom hear *Buongiorno, signore*

(Good morning, Sir) or *Buongiorno, signorina* (Good morning, Miss). To avoid embarrassment, when greeting a woman it is better to just say *Buongiorno!* and not *Buongiorno, signora/signorina* (Good morning, Ma'am/Miss).

It is normal to greet people on the street or on the bus with *Buongiorno!* However, when greeting a group of people it is not necessary to say *buongiorno* to each individual separately. One can just say *Buongiorno a tutti* (Good morning to all).

Buongiorno, Signor Rossi!   Good morning, Mr. Rossi!
Boo-on-JOR-no seen-YOR ROH-SEE
Buongiorno a tutti!   Good morning to all!
Boo-on-JOR-no ah TOOT-tee
Buona giornata!   Have a nice day!
Boo-OH-nah jor-NAH-tah

 Buona notte! *(Boo-OH-nah NOT-teh):* Good night!

When to switch from *buongiorno* to *buon pomeriggio* (good afternoon), then to *buonasera* (good evening) and to *buonanotte* (good night) is a question to which each Italian will give his/her own rule, as the use depends on a personal feeling of time, on the season, etc. *Buongiorno* is used for most of the day, as even in the afternoon it is preferred to *buon pomeriggio*. Even though some native Italians would use *buongiorno* as late as 6:00 P.M., it is probably best to not use this greeting after 5:00 P.M., when stores often reopen for their evening hours.

Buonasera is used for both hello and good-bye in the evening, but it's different from *buona serata*, which is used when someone is leaving for the evening, perhaps to go to a movie.

Buona notte is the expression used when leaving people with whom you have spent the evening or when you know explicitly that a person is going to bed or back home for good.

Buona sera, avvocato.   Good evening, (lawyer).
Boo-OH-nah SEH-rah Ahv-vo-
   CAH-toh
Buona serata!   Have a nice evening!
Boo-OH-nah seh-RAH-tah
Buona notte, Carlo!   Good night, Carlo!
Boo-OH-nah NOT-teh CAR-loh

 Ciao a tutti! *(CHAH-oh ah TOOT-tee):* Hello, everybody!

There is also a difference in formality in the use of the proper greeting. As discussed above, *buongiorno* can be used as a formal or informal way of greeting someone. Italians also use *ciao* or *salve* for informal greetings. When greeting friends, they may shake hands or give each other a kiss on each cheek. This is very common between men as well as women.

Ciao, from the old Venetian dialect meaning "your slave"/"at your service," is a very common form of salutation, but it can be used only informally. It is usually reserved for greeting family members and close friends—for people one knows well. *Ciao* should absolutely not be used with people whom you do not know well, or with older people to whom you want to show respect; the use of *ciao* might offend them. However, it is acceptable to use it in greeting an older family member: *Ciao, nonno* (Hello, grandpa), *Ciao, zia* (Hi, aunt). An interesting use of *ciao* is the title of the movie *Ciao, professore* (the correct form is *Buongiorno, professore*). The title is meant to suggest that

5

the younger generation is much more informal. *Ciao* is also used as a way to say good-bye: *Ciao, ragazzi!* (Good-bye, guys!)

Salve is another informal way of greeting people, although less common than *ciao*. It can be used to express hi or hello but not good-bye. Some native speakers use this salutation when addressing someone with whom they are unsure whether to use the *tu* or the *Lei* form. In actuality, *salve* should be used with people whom you know quite well and with whom you should use the *tu* form: *Salve, come stai?* (Hi, how are you?) At times, however, you may hear: *Salve, come sta?* In such instances, if not sure whether to be formal or informal in your response, always use the more polite expression *Buongiorno, come sta?*

Ciao, ragazzi.	Hi/Bye, guys.
CHAH-oh rah-GAHT-tsee	
Ciao, Maria!	Hi/Bye, Maria!
CHAH-oh Mah-REE-ah	
Ciao, ragazze!	Hi/Bye, girls!
CHAH-oh rah-GAHT-tseh	
Salve, Mario.	Hello, Mario.
SAHL-veh MAH-ree-oh	

 Arrivederci! *(Ahr-ree-veh-DAIR-chee):* Good-bye!

The word *arrivederci* (literally, 'Til we see each other again") has the meaning of good-bye. Similar to *ciao*, *arrivederci* is colloquially taking the place of the formal *arrivederLa*, especially when saying good-bye to a group of people.

While on the phone, Italians may also use *Arrisentirci!* (Literally, 'Til we hear each other again! / Until next time! / Goodbye for now!)

As a form of salutation, in movies or written documents, Italians may use the word *addio*, which is meant as a more permanent or final good-bye. In spoken language, *addio* is considered archaic.

Arrivederci a tutti!	Good-bye to all!
Ahr-ree-veh-DAIR-chee ah TOOT-tee	
ArrivederLa, ingegnere.	Good-bye, (engineer).
Ahr-ree-veh-DAIR-lah in-jeh-NYEH-reh	
Bye-bye.	Good-bye.
Bye-bye	
Addio per sempre!	Good-bye forever!
Ahd-DEE-oh pair SEHM-preh	

 A presto! *(Ah PREH-sto):* See you soon!

Other forms of salutation meaning "good-bye" are: *A domani!, Ci vediamo!, A presto!* These expressions are not very formal and are normally used with people one knows well. *A domani!* and *Ci vediamo!* are usually used if you already know you are going to meet the person somewhere very soon or if you usually meet him/her somewhere. *A presto!* is, instead, very vague in regard to the time frame. Note that *A presto!* is often used to end a letter or an e-mail message. In addition, it is quite common to use the informal closing expressions *arrisentirci* or *ci sentiamo domani/più tardi* ('til later/tomorrow). The latter expression could also be used in Internet chat rooms, when the exchanges occur frequently and regularly.

Other forms of good-bye salutation are:

A dopo!   See you later!
Ah DOH-po

Ci vediamo tra poco!   See you in a while!
Chee veh-dee-AH-mo trah PO-co

Stammi bene!   Keep well!
STAHM-mee BEH-neh

Ciao ciao!   Good-bye!
CHAH-oo CHAH-oo

Alla prossima!   'Til the next time!
AHL-lah PROS-see-mah

 Come va, Carlo? *(CO-meh vah CAHR-lo):* How's it going, Carlo?

As we have seen previously, to ask someone the question "How are you?" use *Come sta?* in a polite setting and *Come stai?* in an informal setting. The expression *Come va?*, even though very colloquial, could be used in both formal and informal settings: *Come va, Carlo?* or *Come va, professore?* In a very informal and colloquial setting, Italians will often use the impersonal pronoun *si* before *va*: *Come si va, Carlo?* or *Come si va, professore?*

Come sta, signora Lavezzi?   How are you, Mrs. Lavezzi?
CO-meh stah seen-YO-rah
   Lah-VETS-see

Come vanno le cose?   How are things going?
CO-meh VAHN-no leh CO-seh

Come si va, ragazzi?   How's it going, guys?
CO-meh see vah rah-GAHTS-tsee

Le presento il dottor Carli. *(Leh preh-ZEN-toh eel dot-TOR CAHR-lee):* This is Dr. Carli.

When introducing people, depending on the situation, one needs to be careful in using the *Lei* or *tu* form. Therefore, use *Le presento il dottor Carli* for formal introductions and *Ti presento Mario* for informal introductions. When introducing a person to more than one individual, *Vi presento* is used in both formal and informal situations: *Vi presento il professor Lavia* or *Vi presento Mario*. In any situation, it is also acceptable to introduce someone without using a form of the verb *presentare* at all; just use *Il professor Dini*, or *Carlo*. The entire action is accompanied by a handshake (a firm handshake), and it is followed by the formal/informal *Piacere* (Nice to meet you.), which could be replaced by a more wordy formal response: *Piacere di fare la Sua conoscenza!/Piacere della conoscenza!/Molto lieto!* (masc.) / *Molto lieta!* (fem.)

In formal situations, at the end of a conversation (when people are about to go their separate ways), one would reiterate, accompanied with the handshake: *Piacere!/Piacere della conoscenza!/Piacere di aver fatto la Sua conoscenza!* A response to the sayings above is *Il piacere è mio!* (The pleasure is mine!) These expressions, however, are becoming more unusual.

At times, among young people in very informal situations today, the word *piacere* may not even be used with introductions.

In cases when you may need to make your own introduction, depending on the context, you would use: *Mi chiamo Luigi/Luigi Rossi/ Rossi*. If it is the other person who is presenting himself/herself first, just follow his/her presentation style.

Marco Calvi. Piacere. Marco Calvi. Nice to meet you.
MAHR-co CAL-vee peeah-CHEH-reh

Mamma e papà, vi presento il mio amico Luigi.
MAHM-mah eh pah-PAH vee preh-ZEN-toh eel MEE-oh ah-MEE-co Loo-EE-gee

Mom and Dad, I would like to introduce to you my friend Luigi.

Franco, Carlo. Carlo, Franco.
FRAHN-co CAHR-lo CAHR-lo FRAHN-co

Franco, this is Carlo. Carlo, this is Franco.

Dottore, Le presento i miei genitori.
Dot-TOH-reh Leh preh-ZEN-toh ee mee-AY jeh-nee-TOH-ree

Doctor, I would like to introduce you to my parents.

 Benvenuto! *(Behn-veh-NOO-toh):* Welcome!

Italians are well known for making you feel welcome and part of their home. If someone is meeting you at the airport in Italy, you will be welcomed with *Benvenuto!/Benvenuta in Italia.* If you are a guest in someone's home, you will be welcomed with *Benvenuto/Benvenuta nella nostra casa!* (Welcome to our home!)

Chapter 2

Good Manners

 Un caffè, per favore. *(Oon caf-FEH pair fah-VO-reh):* A coffee, please.

Don't expect your manners to have the same results in Italy as they do in North America. For example, the polite words *grazie, prego,* and *scusi* are easily recognized as some of the most important words to learn, but they are often thought to be interchangeable with their English counterparts. A key aspect of learning Italian manners is to know how and when to use the *formule di cortesia* (polite expressions). The *formule di cortesia* are useful both as Italian expressions and as ways of using nonverbal communication effectively.

Our own manners in our own country are instinctive, and we often do not realize that we have been using manners all our lives. If you are not Italian, though, you probably have not been using "Italian manners" all your life. Italian manners may even seem like an oxymoron to outsiders, but learning them opens the door to understanding and enjoying Italian culture and people.

The Italian magic courtesy words can at first seem deceptively easy because they seem to be straightforward equivalents of the magic words in English. In reality, though, it's a lot easier to learn the Italian formulas than to know how and when to use them. Context is important in determining whether a *formula di cortesia* is really polite or not. Consider the various meanings of the expressions that will follow in this chapter.

Per piacere!/Per favore!/Per cortesia! are interchangeable expressions, even though *Per favore!* is most commonly used, followed by *Per piacere!*, with *Per cortesia!* a distant third.

Per favore is an amazingly versatile expression. Because it is so versatile, *per favore* is used much more often and in many different contexts than the word "please" is used in English. *Per favore* is also used to get someone's attention. So, *Per favore! Un caffè, per favore!* would be "Waiter! Coffee, please." Saying *per favore* works better and is more polite than snapping fingers when trying to get the attention of a salesperson or a waiter, but it's the same idea.

Per favore can also be used as an opener when asking directions. Again, you can use it twice: the first time to get someone's attention and the second time to be polite. *Per favore! Potrebbe dirmi come arrivare a Piazza Duomo, per favore?* (I beg your pardon. Could you please tell me how to get to Piazza Duomo?)

Per favore is also sometimes used in a unique way in addition to the previous meanings. Consider the following sentence, pronounced with an annoyed tone of voice: *Ma per favore, non dica stupidaggini!* (Please, stop saying nonsense!) Sometimes, simply *Ma per favore...!* works just as well.

Potrebbe indicarmi dov'è la stazione della metropolitana, per favore?

Could you please tell me where the subway station is?

Po-TREB-beh een-dee-CAHR-mee doh-VEH lah stah-tsee-OH-neh DEL-lah meh-tro-po-lee-TAH-nah pair fah-VO-reh

Per cortesia, sii gentile; mi aiuti.

Please, be kind; help me.

Pair cor-teh-ZEE-ah SEE-ee jen-TEE-leh mee aye-OO-tee

Per piacere, potrebbe dirmi che ore sono?

Could you please tell me what time it is?

Pair peeah-CHEH-reh po-TREB-beh DEER-mee keh OH-reh SO-no

Potrebbe farmi la cortesia di validarmi questo biglietto?

Would you be so kind as to validate this ticket for me?

Po-TREB-beh FAR-mee lah cor-teh-ZEE-ah dee va-lee-DAHR-mee QUEH-sto beel-YET-toh

 Molto gentile, grazie. *(MOHL-toh jen-TEE-leh GRAH-tsee-eh):* That's very kind, thank you.

When Italian children forget to say "thank you," they are prompted with *Come si dice?* (What do you say?) Thanking people is a form of courtesy common to every culture and language. This is why there are many different ways to express gratitude in Italian, as well as in other languages. At times, a simple gesture will do it; other times a smile; or you may want to express it with a gift or a card. The most immediate way is with words, while the action is being done. A simple *grazie*

will do the trick, but there are many Italian expressions used to say "thank you very much"/"thanks a million": *mille grazie* or *grazie mille*, *tante grazie* or *grazie tante*, *grazie infinite* or *infinite grazie*, or *molte grazie*. Or if you prefer, *grazie di cuore* (a heart-felt thank you) or *grazie di tutto* (thank you for everything), *sì, grazie* (yes, thank you), or *no, grazie* (no, thank you). Below are some less-simple verbal expressions of gratitude:

Grazie del Suo aiuto.	Thank you for your help.
GRAH-tsee-eh del SOO-oh aye-OO-toh	
Ti/Le sono assai riconoscente.	I am very grateful.
Tee/Leh SO-no ass-AYE ree-co-no-SHEN-teh	
Ti/La ringrazio infinitamente.	Thank you very much indeed.
Tee/Lah reen-GRAH-tsee-oh een-FEE-nee-tah-MEN-teh	
Non ho parole per ringraziarti/ ringraziarLa.	I have no words to thank you.
Nohn oh pah-RO-leh pair reen-GRAH-tsee-ahr-tee/ reen-GRAH-tsee-ahr-Lah	

 Prego! *(PREH-go):* You're welcome!

Italians normally respond to *grazie* with the very polite and simple *Prego!* (You're welcome!) If you prefer to be more verbose, you may respond by somehow minimizing what you have done, implying that a thank you is not really necessary: *È il minimo che possa fare* (It's the least I could do), *È poca cosa* (It's really nothing/the smallest of things),

Si figuri!/Figurati! (Don't worry, it's really nothing), *Non c'è/c'era bisogno di ringraziarmi* (There is/was no need to thank me), or *Dovere!* (It's/It was my duty!)

Di niente! It's nothing!/No problem!
Dee nee-EN-teh

È molto gentile da parte Sua! It's very kind of you!
Eh MOHL-toh jen-TEE-leh dah
    PAHR-teh SOO-ah

Grazie a te! Thank *you*!
GRAH-tsee-eh ah teh

È solo un pensierino! It's just a small thought!
Eh SO-lo oon pen-see-eh-REE-no

 Scusi!/Scusa! *(SCOO-zee/SCOO-zah):* I beg your pardon!

Scusi!/Scusa! means "Excuse me!"/"I'm sorry for what I did!"/"I apologize!" *Scusi* is more formal than *scusa.* It can't be said too often. Using *scusi* is also a polite and effective way to start a request. To ask for directions, start by saying *Scusi!* to get a person's attention. Then continue with the request: *Per favore, potrebbe dirmi come arrivare a Piazza Duomo?* (Excuse me! Please, could you tell me how to get to Piazza Duomo?)

Scusi!/Scusa! can also mean "Please let me get by!" or "Excuse me for something I'm about to do!" such as squeeze past to get to a seat at the movies.

Finally, a classic introduction to disagreeing with someone is *Scusa, ma ti sbagli!* or *Scusi, ma si sbaglia!* (Pardon me for saying so, but you're wrong!) In this context, *scusi/scusa* is not really polite at all, but mock-polite.

15

Posso? is very useful as a way of announcing an otherwise aggressive intention in a way that sounds polite: "May I?"/"Do you mind?" It may simply mean "Do you mind if I sit here?" But it could also mean "I'm going to sit here," "Do you mind if I smoke?," or "You'll have to move your coat." The typical response is *Prego!/Faccia pure!* (No problem!)

Permesso? is used to make one's way through a crowd and has the meaning of "Please, let me (may I) go by!" The answer, if any, would be *Prego!* The expression *Permesso?* is also used when knocking at a door and in this case is equivalent to "May I come in?" The answer is *Prego!* if the door is open or *Avanti!* if the door is closed.

Scusi, dov'è l'Hotel Excelsior?
SCOO-zee doh-VEH lo-TEL
Ex-chel-SEE-or

Excuse me, where is the Excelsior Hotel?

Scusi… Permesso… dovrei scendere alla prossima fermata.
SCOO-zee Pair-MES-so doh-VRAY
SHEN-deh-reh AHL-lah
PROS-see-mah fair-MAH-tah

Excuse me . . . Excuse me . . . I need to get off at the next stop.

Posso? Le dispiace se mi siedo qui?
POS-so Leh dee-spee-AH-cheh
seh mee see-EH-doh quee

May I? Do you mind if I sit here?

Permesso? C'è nessuno in casa?
Pair-MES-so Cheh nes-SOO-no
een CAH-zah

Excuse me? Is anyone home?

Prego! *(PREH-go):* After you, please!

As discussed above, in reply to *grazie,* Italians say *Prego!* to mean *You're welcome.* However, like *per favore* and *scusa/scusi, prego* is another classic *espressione di cortesia* with a flexible meaning. Depending on the situation, *Prego!* can also mean "Please!" as in "After you" or "Please, go ahead." If used in response to *Scusa!/Scusi!, Prego!* means "No problem!"

However, *prego* can be said with annoyance also, as in *(Ti/La) prego, basta!* (For goodness sake, cut it out!) This is another example of the importance of context in determining whether an *espressione di cortesia* is really polite or not.

Prego! (when meant as "After you") is always polite to say at a doorway. And the correct reply is usually, *No, prego!* or *Dopo di Lei.* ("No, please." or "After you.") Who goes through the doorway first is determined by a certain hierarchy: women before men, older women before younger women, and so forth.

Prego, dopo di Lei!	After you, please!
PREH-go DOH-po dee Lay	
Prego, entri pure!	Please, come in!
PREH-go EN-tree POO-reh	
Ti prego, Carletto, finiscila!	Please, Carletto, stop!
Tee PREH-go Cahr-LET-toh fee-NEE-shee-lah	
Prego, faccia pure!	Please, go ahead!
PREH-go FAH-cha POO-reh	

Mi dispiace! *(Mee dee-spee-AH-cheh)*: I'm sorry!

Mi dispiace, like its English equivalent, "I'm sorry," is a very flexible expression and will acquire its meaning depending on the situation and context as well as tone of voice used. In a sad tone of voice, it could indicate sorrow: a loss in the family, a health- or job-related issue. When the expression is used by itself with a firm tone of voice, it becomes another way of saying no to something. Other times, when the expression is followed or could be followed by "but" (*ma*), it might express regret.

Mi dispiace. Condoglianze!
Mee dee-spee-AH-cheh
    Kohn-dohl-YAHNT-seh

I'm sorry. My condolences!

**Mi dispiace! Ti auguro una
    pronta guarigione!**
Mee dee-spee-AH-cheh Tee
    AH-oo-goo-roh OO-nah
    PRON-tah goo-ah-ree-JO-neh

I'm sorry! I wish you a quick recovery!

Mi dispiace, ma non parlo italiano.
Mee dee-spee-AH-cheh mah nohn
    PAHR-lo ee-tahl-ee-AH-no

I am sorry, but I do not speak Italian.

Mi dispiace! Non puoi uscire!
Mee dee-spee-AH-cheh Nohn
    poo-OY oo-SHEE-reh

No! You cannot go out!

 Posso offrirti un caffè? *(POS-so of-FREER-tee oon cahf-FEH)*: May I offer you a coffee?

If you have something that can be shared, you share with everyone present. To be inclusive is one of the Italian ways to be polite.

In Italy it is very common to meet friends at a local bar (the Italian "bar" is the equivalent of an American café, frequented by people of all ages, where one can play cards, have breakfast or coffee, play video games, have a drink, etc.). When one meets a friend, it is customary to offer him/her a coffee or a drink at the local bar: *Posso offrirti un caffè?* (May I offer you a coffee?); *Vieni che ti offro un caffè!* (Come and I will offer you a coffee!) If one is not offered something, he/she may be offended.

It is polite for guests to argue a bit with someone who wants to pay the bill, even if the invitation was made by you. In this case, you may want to say: *Non ci pensare neanche/nemmeno!* (Don't even think about it!/I wouldn't dream of letting you!) Similarly, if you are the invited guest, and you want to pay, say: *Permetti che offro/pago io!* (Allow me to pay!) Often you will need all your skills and tricks to be allowed to pay in such situations. In case of a repeated invitation, you might stress that this time you want to pay: *Questa volta pago io, però!* (This time it is my turn to pay, though!)

Together with coffee, Italians love to offer cigarettes. In Italy one never lights a cigarette without first offering one to everyone present. This habit is, however, slightly changing due to the antismoking campaign.

Prendi un caffè?
PREHN-dee oon cahf-FEH

Would you like a coffee?

Cosa posso offrirti?
CO-sah POS-so ohf-FREER-tee

What can I offer you?

Cosa prendi?
CO-sa PREHN-dee

What are you taking?

No, pago io!
No PAH-go EE-oh

No, I'll pay!

Ti aspettiamo a cena da noi, stasera! *(Tee as-pet-tee-AH-mo ah CHEH-nah dah noy stah-SEH-rah):* Please join us for supper tonight!

Italians' hospitality is even more evident when they have guests in their homes. For Italians, guests are sacred and they love feeding them. One of the first things offered in an Italian home is wine and a delicious meal.

A polite way to make it clear that you intend to pay is to use the verb *invitare* when you make a plan. *Ti invito* means both "I invite you" and "I'll pay." You wouldn't use the verb *invitare* in that context if you weren't intending to pay. If someone says *Ti invito*, the reply could be *È gentile da parte tua* (That's very nice of you) or *Sei troppo gentile* (You're very kind/too kind).

Certain polite responses are automatic. If you have people over at your place and it is time for them to go, even if you are ready for your guests to leave, you are expected to say *Di già?* (Already?) or *Ve ne andate già?* (Are you already leaving?)

If you are not free to accept an invitation, it's polite to suggest that *sarà per un'altra volta* (it will be for another time) so as not to seem too abrupt. It's good to express reciprocity for good wishes such as *Buon appetito* (Enjoy your meal! Literally, Good appetite!) by replying, *Altrettanto* or *Grazie altrettante*.

Ci fa molto piacere.	We're delighted.
Chee fah MOHL-toh peeah-CHEH-reh	
Restate ancora un po': non c'è fretta.	Stay a bit longer: there is no hurry.
Reh-STAH-teh ahn-CO-rah oon PO nohn cheh FRET-tah	

Volentieri./Con piacere.
Vol-ehn-tee-EH-ree/Kohn
  peeah-CHEH-reh

With pleasure.

Che serata eccezionale!
Keh seh-RAH-tah eh-chets-
  see-oh-NAH-leh

What a terrific evening!

 Come stanno i tuoi? *(CO-meh STAHN-no ee too-OY):*
How are your parents/family?

Good manners could also be shown by asking people about their loved ones or by making them feel welcome. For example, for Italians it is important to talk about the health of the family; they will definitely appreciate if you ask: *Tutti bene a casa?* (Is everyone well at home?) First thing in the morning it is OK to ask a friend if he or she has slept well (*Dormito bene?*), while at night you could wish him or her a good night and sweet dreams. (*Buona notte! Sogni d'oro!*)

There are many occasions to be solicitous to other people: to make them feel welcome, to show care, to be helpful; in other words, to display your good manners. Here are a few expressions: *Benvenuti!* (Welcome!), *Che piacere rivederti*! (It's good to see you again!), *Buona permanenza!* (Have a nice stay!)

State comodi.
STAH-teh CO-mo-dee

Don't get up.

Fate come a casa vostra.
FAH-teh CO-meh ah CAH-zah
  VO-strah

Make yourself at home.

Attenzione allo scalino.
Aht-ten-tsee-OH-neh AHL-lo
  scah-LEE-no

Watch your step.

Serve qualcosa?	Do you need anything?/Do you
SEHR-veh quahl-CO-zah	have everything you need?

 Salute! *(Sah-LOO-teh):* Bless you!/Gesundheit!

Good manners could also be used to minimize someone's embarrassing moment: a false step, dropping something, sneezing, etc. If, for example, someone is apologizing for something clumsy, you may want to minimize the embarrassment by saying: *Ma non è successo niente!* (Nothing happened!/No harm done!) If someone has just broken a glass or spilled and stained something, you might say: *Niente di grave* (It's nothing). If the person is continuously apologizing, you may want to say: *Non te la prendere* (Don't worry about it) or *Non ci pensare più!* (Don't think/worry about it anymore!) As you can see, the expressions for responding to a faux pas tend to be in the negative form because they are about not worrying.

When a person sneezes, one would say *Salute!* ("Gesundheit!" Literally, "Health!") Remember that when drinking, *Salute!* also means "Cheers!" (Literally, "To your health!")

Non fa niente.	It's nothing.
Non fah nee-EHN-teh	
Non ti preoccupare.	Don't worry.
Non tee preh-oc-coo-PAH-reh	
Nessun problema.	No problem.
Nehs-SOON pro-BLEH-mah	
È normale./Si capisce.	That's understandable.
Eh nor-MAH-leh/See cah-PEE-sheh	

Auguri! *(Ah-oo-GOO-ree):* Congratulations!

Expressing approval for something, congratulating someone for his or her achievements, expressing best wishes, and complimenting someone are all indications of good manners.

Mi congratulo!	Congratulations!/I congratulate you!
Mee con-GRAH-too-lo	
Ben fatto!	Well done!/Very good!
Behn FAHT-toh	
Sei in forma!	You look fit!
Say een FOR-mah	
Ti sta proprio bene!	That looks very good on you!
Tee stah PRO-pree-oh BEH-neh	

 Mi dispiace per il ritardo! *(Mee dee-spee-AH-cheh pair eel ree-TAHR-doh):* My apologies for being late!

For Evelyn Waugh *"La puntualità è la virtù dell'annoiato"*; for others *"La puntualità è l'anima del commercio."* For Italians in general, fifteen minutes late is considered ideal, and there's a special expression for being fifteen minutes late: *il quarto d'ora accademico*, meaning the "traditional fifteen minutes late." Arriving more than fifteen minutes late is considered rude. If you are more than ten minutes late, it's polite to offer an excuse. If you are more than twenty minutes late, you must. Some of the most common phrases to start a polite excuse with are: *Scusate per il ritardo, ma...* (My apologies for being late, but . . .), *Scusate, ma...* (My apologies, but . . .), or *Mi dispiace, ma...* (I am sorry, but . . .). Useful and acceptable explanations are: *Ho sbagliato indirizzo* (I had the wrong address), *Ho sbagliato strada* (I took a wrong turn), *Ho perso l'autobus/il treno* (I missed the bus/train), *Ho preso l'autobus*

sbagliato (I took the wrong bus), *Ho perso la coincidenza* (I missed the train/flight/bus connection), *Mi sono perso* (I got lost), and *Non conoscevo la strada* (I didn't know the way).

Ho dovuto aspettare a lungo per un tassì. OH doh-VOO-toh as-pet-TAH-reh ah LOON-go pair oon tahs-SEE	I had to wait a long time for a taxi.
Ho dovuto rispondere ad una telefonata all'ultimo minuto. Oh doh-VOO-toh ree-SPON-deh-reh ahd OO-nah teh-leh-fo-NAH-tah ahl-LOOL-tee-mo mee-NOO-toh	I had a last-minute phone call.
L'orologio s'è fermato. Lo-ro-LO-jo seh fair-MAH-toh	My watch stopped.
C'era molto traffico. CHEH-rah MOL-toh TRAHF-fee-co	There was a lot of traffic.

 Buon divertimento! *(Boo-ON dee-vair-tee-MEHN-toh):* Have a good time!

Expressions with *buon* and *buono, buona,* etc., are easy to understand but counterintuitive for Americans to use, because they cannot be literally translated. Fortunately, we already use the French expression *Bon voyage!* in English. Using *Bon voyage!* as a model for Italian *buon* expressions will help you break the habit of literally translating into Italian the English structure *Have a . . . .* For example, *Buone vacanze!* (Happy holidays!) is used much more often than *Fate delle buone vacanze!* (Have happy holidays!)

Buon onomastico is used to wish someone a happy name's day; since in Italy many people are named after saints, the *onomastico* is celebrated on the feast of the saint with the same name. Similarly, because Italy is mainly a Catholic country, *Buone feste!* (Literally, "Good feasts!" or "Good celebration!") is strictly used at Christmas and at Easter time. Italians also say *Buon Natale!* (Merry Christmas!), *Buona Pasqua!* (Happy Easter!), or *Buon Anno!* (Happy New Year!)

To wish someone good luck, more than *buona fortuna*, Italians use *In bocca al lupo* (literally, "In the wolf's mouth"). The appropriate response to this is *Crepi!* or *Crepi il lupo!* (May the wolf die!), even though at times you will hear *Grazie.*

Buon compleanno/onomastico!	Happy birthday! Happy "name day"!
Boo-ON com-pleh-AHN-no/ oh-no-MAH-stee-co	
Buon viaggio!	Have a pleasant journey! / Have a nice trip!
Boo-ON vee-AHD-jo	
Buon appetito!	Enjoy your meal!
Boo-ON ahp-peh-TEE-toh	
Buona permanenza!	Have a nice stay!
Boo-OH-nah pair-mah-NEHN-tsah	

Chapter 3

Money Matters

 Per favore, potrebbe dirmi dove posso trovare una banca? *(Pair fah-VO-reh po-TREB-beh DEER-mee DOH-veh POS-so tro-VAH-reh OO-nah BAN-cah):* Could you please tell me where to find a bank?

Bank business hours can vary, depending on the bank and on the city. Normally, banks are open Monday through Friday, from 8:30 A.M. to 1:30 P.M. and then from 3:30 P.M. to 4:30 P.M. In the airports, train stations, or in tourist areas, business hours are normally nonstop from 8:30 A.M. to 4:00 P.M.

Banks and post offices are the most reliable places to change money and traveler's checks, and generally they offer the best exchange rates and charge the lowest commissions.

Don't be surprised at the level of security in Italian banks. To enter a bank, you must often go through two sets of security doors. You will also find that the number of clients inside the bank may be limited to a few at a time.

Please remember that when dealing with bank, post office, or exchange office employees, store clerks, or shop owners, or when just asking for information, the use of the *Lei* form is imperative.

A che ora apre/chiude la banca?	At what time does the bank
Ah keh OH-rah Ah-preh/	open/close?
KEEOO-deh la BAN-ca	

 Scusi, dove potrei trovare un bancomat? *(SCOO-zee DOH-veh po-TRAY tro-VAH-reh oon BAN-co-maht):* Pardon me, where could I find an ATM?

As in North America, Bancomat machines (ATMs) are available even in small towns and are always open. You will often find them just outside a bank or inside the first set of security doors, which you may open by inserting your ATM card. Your North American ATM card is also valid for the Bancomat, and transactions can be done entirely in English. The exchange rate is set by the value of the currency for the day; please note that a small fee of two to three dollars (set by your bank) is charged for each transaction. A withdrawal limit of 500 euros per transaction usually applies.

 Scusi, dove potrei trovare l'ufficio del cambio? *(SCOO-zee DOH-veh po-TRAY tro-VAH-reh loo-FEE-cho del CAHM-bee-oh):* Pardon me, where could I find an exchange office?

Except for international airports, major train stations, and tourist areas, it is not easy to locate an exchange office in a small town or even a major city. The best place to exchange money is at a bank or a post office; as mentioned above, they offer the best rates and charge the lowest commission. In tourist areas, it may be possible to exchange money in hotels, stores, department stores, and even in tourist souvenir booths. When this is the case, be sure to ask about the exchange rate (*il cambio*) and the commission fee (*la commissione*).

A quanto sta il dollaro?
Ah QUAHN-toh stah eel dol-LAH-ro
What is the exchange rate for the dollar?

Vorrei cambiare dei traveler's cheque.
Vor-RAY cahm-bee-AH-reh day TRAH-veh-lers chek
I would like to exchange some traveler's checks.

Quanto è la commissione?
QUAHN-toh eh lah com-mis-see-OH-neh
How much is the commission?

 Vorrei cambiare duecento dollari in euro. *(Vor-RAY cahm-bee-AH-reh doo-eh-CHEHN-toh DOL-lah-ree een EH-oo-ro):* I would like to exchange two hundred dollars into euros.

The monetary unit in Italy and in most of the European Union is the euro. In Italy the euro was introduced on January 1, 2002, replacing the lira. Euro banknotes have the following denominations: 5, 10, 20, 50, 100, 200, and 500 euros; coins come in 1, 2, 5, 10, 20, and 50 cents and 1 and 2 euros. One side of each coin features the same design for all European nations (a map of the European Union and transversal lines with the stars of the European flag) and the other side represents a single member state. Euros (coins and bills) can be used anywhere in the European Union.

The graphic symbol of the euro (€) was inspired by the Greek letter epsilon (as the first letter of "Europe" and as a homage to Greece as the cradle of European civilization); two parallel lines cross the image, as a symbol of currency stability.

Note that the word *euro* is invariable in the plural. The euro is divided into *centesimi* (sing. *centesimo*).

Finally, please also note that English and Italian have opposite uses for the comma and the period within numbers: *Io ho 2.000 dollari* versus "I have 2,000 dollars."

Per favore, potrebbe darmi dei biglietti di piccolo taglio/ di grosso taglio/da dieci euro?	Could you please give me small/large/ten-euro bills?

Pair fah-VO-reh po-TREB-beh
DAHR-mee day beel-YET-tee dee
PEEK-co-lo TAHL-yo/dee GROS-so
TAHL-yo/dah dee-EH-chee
EH-oo-ro

Pago con la carta di credito. *(PAH-go kohn lah CAHR-tah dee CREH-dee-to):* I will pay with my credit card.

Major credit cards are commonly accepted in Italy, even in small towns. Traveler's checks are not as commonly accepted as a form of payment, however, and there may be a commission fee. When paying with a credit card or with traveler's checks, you might be asked to show a personal identification document (*documento di riconoscimento*). Here are some expressions to use on such occasions:

Accetta dei traveler's cheque?
At-CHEHT-tah day TRA-veh-lers chek

Do you accept traveler's checks?

Ecco la carta di credito.
EHC-co lah CAHR-tah dee
   CREH-dee-toh

Here is my credit card.

Ecco il passaporto/la patente
   di guida.
EHC-co eel pahs-sah-POR-toh/
   lah pah-TEHN-teh dee goo-EE-dah

Here is my passport/my driver's
   license.

 Vorrei fare un bonifico bancario. *(Voh-RAY FAH-reh oon boh-NEE-fee-coh ban-CAH-ree-oh):* I would like to make a bank transfer.

To send money to someone outside Italy, make a *bonifico bancario* (money transfer). You could also buy a *vaglia postale* (money order), which you must mail yourself. One of the safest ways to send or receive money while traveling is to use the online system PayPal.

Vorrei comprare un vaglia
   postale.
Voh-RAY cohm-PRAH-reh oon
   VAHL-llee-yah poh-STAH-leh

I would like to buy a money order.

Chapter 4

Hotels

 L'albergo Aurora, per favore. *(Lahl-BEHR-go Ah-oo-RO-rah pair fah-VO-reh)*: To the Hotel Aurora, please.

This phrase could be useful to tell a taxi driver to take you to your hotel. However, as in North America, large hotels have service booths in the major airports and train stations.

Obviously the price range varies, depending on the period of travel, the city, and the choice of hotel, but generally prices are quite expensive. It is common in Italy to find monastery/convent hotels— actual monasteries located in idyllic and historical locations, which are informally rated as the equivalent of three- to four-star hotels. Their prices vary, but they are generally very affordable: an average of 40 to 50 euros for a single and 80 to 90 euros for a double. For a three-star hotel the average price is 110 euros; for a modest *pensione* 80 euros.

Scusi, potrebbe indicarmi un albergo/una pensione qui vicino, per favore?
SCOO-zee po-TREB-beh een-dee-CAHR-mee oon ahl-BEHR-go/ OO-na pehn-see-OH-neh kwee vee-CHEE-no pair fah-VO-reh

Pardon me, could you please point me to a hotel/*pensione* close by?

Scusi, potrebbe indicarmi come arrivare all'albergo Aurora, per favore?
SCOO-zee po-TREB-beh een-dee-CAHR-mee CO-meh ahr-ree-VAH-reh ahl-lahl-BEHR-go Ah-oo-RO-rah pair fah-VO-reh

Pardon me, could you please tell me how to get to the Hotel Aurora?

 C'è un buon bed and breakfast vicino? *(CHEH oon boo-ON bed and breakfast quee vee-CHEE-noh):* Is there a nice bed and breakfast nearby?

Tourism is Italy's largest asset, and therefore there is a great variety of accommodations throughout the country: from luxurious hotels and villas to resort villages, from family-run *pensioni* to youth hostels, from *agriturismo* sites to campgrounds. If you are on a tight budget, there are many bed-and-breakfast places and *albergo/ostello della gioventù* (youth hostels).

C'è un albergo della gioventù in questa città?
CHEH oon al-BEHR-goh dehl-la jo-vehn-TOO een QUE-sta cheet-TAH

Is there a youth hostel in this city?

Vorrei fare una prenotazione. *(Voh-RAY FAH-reh OO-na preh-no-tah-tsee-OH-neh):* I would like to make a reservation.

Finding accommodations during the tourist season in Italy, especially in tourist areas, can be very problematic; make your hotel reservations well ahead of time. If it was not possible to reserve ahead, ask someone: *Scusi, potrebbe indicarmi un albergo/una pensione qui vicino?* (Excuse me, could you please suggest a hotel close by?) If you get lost after visiting the city or going to an excursion, and you are near the hotel, ask someone: *Scusi, potrebbe indicarmi come arrivare all'albergo Aurora?* (Excuse me, could you please tell me how to get to the albergo Aurora?) or, simply, *L'albergo Aurora, per favore* (Albergo Aurora, please).

For reservation purposes, hotels request a proof of identification (normally a passport); small hotels might ask you to leave the key to your room while going out for the day.

Vorrei prenotare una singola/ doppia (or **matrimoniale**) **per due notti.**
Vor-RAY preh-no-TAH-reh OO-nah SEEN-go-lah/DOP-pee-ah (*or* mah-tree-mo-nee-AH-leh) pair DOO-eh NOT-tee

I would like to reserve a single/ double room for two nights.

Mi dispiace, ma devo cancellare la mia prenotazione.
Me dee-spee-AH-cheh mah DEH-voh can-chehl-LAH-reh la MEE-ah preh-no-tah-tsee-OH-neh

I'm sorry, but I need to cancel my reservation.

Ha una camera per una notte/per stasera? *(Ah OO-nah CAH-meh-rah pair OO-nah NOT-teh/pair stah-SEH-rah):* Do you have a room available for one night/tonight?

Hotel rooms in Italy are generally comparable to those in North America. Even family-run hotels and monastery-hotels are comparable to American standards; generally, they all have a private bathroom (*il bagno*), bathtub (*il bagno*) and/or shower (*la doccia*), television (*la televisone),* and a comfortably sized room (*la camera*). However, to avoid unpleasant surprises, especially with smaller venues, it is always a good idea to ask about what's in a room and to check the room itself. If you wish, it is also a good idea to point out that you want a nonsmoking room (*una camera per non fumatori*).

Desidererei avere una camera tranquilla/con veduta panoramica/che dia sul cortile/ che non dia sulla strada principale.	I would like a quiet room/a room with a view/a room that overlooks the courtyard/a room that does not face the main street.
Deh-see-deh-REH-ray ah-VEH-reh OO-nah CAH-meh-rah trahn-QUEEL-lah/kohn veh-DOO-tah pah-no-RAH-mee-cah/keh DEE-ah sool cor-TEE-leh/keh nohn DEE-ah SOOL-lah STRAH-dah preen-chee-PAH-leh	

La colazione è inclusa? *(Lah co-lah-tsee-OH-neh eh een-CLOO-zah):* Is breakfast included?

Breakfast is often included in the price in many Italian hotels and *pensioni*, but be sure to ask anyway. It is usually a rich breakfast buffet for all tastes: *uova* (eggs), *pancetta* (bacon), *burro* (butter), *marmellata* (jam), croissants, *panini* (rolls), *cioccolata calda* (hot chocolate), *formaggio* (cheese), Nutella, *tè* (tea), regular coffee, milk, espresso, cappuccino, *caffellatte*, *latte*, and many other items. Many hotels also cater to clients with celiac disease and offer a gluten-free breakfast. Breakfast is normally served between 7:00 A.M. and 10:00 A.M.

A che ora viene servita la colazione?
Ah keh OH-rah vee-EH-neh sair-VEE-tah lah co-lah-tsee-OH-neh

At what time is breakfast served?

 Dove posso parcheggiare la macchina? *(DOH-veh POS-so pahr-kehd-JA-reh lah MAHK-kee-nah):* Where can I park my car?

Parking is available in big hotels but you must pay extra. Quite a few smaller hotels and *pensioni* might offer free parking.

Many hotels, including small ones, also include in their price a free in-room Internet connection. However, in some hotels there is an extra cost. Also, many hotels offer free Internet services in the lobby.

C'è il collegamento Internet in camera?
CHEH eel col-leh-gah-MEHN-toh EEN-tair-neht een CAH-meh-rah?

Is an Internet connection available in the room?

Come si fa a regolare il climatizzatore? *(CO-meh see fah ah reh-go-LAH-re eel clee-mah-teets-sah-TO-reh):* Can the air-conditioning/heating be adjusted?

Adjusting the air-conditioning/heating temperature in any hotel room in Europe or in North America can often become a real challenge. The sentences below will assist you when asking for help. If there is no air-conditioning, or if it is too hot or too cold, ask to be moved to another room. The location of your room might contribute not only to the temperature in it but also to the level of noise you are exposed to. Be sure to consider that when opting to change rooms. To save energy, some small hotels might use a system which should be manually activated as soon as you open the door to your room. Once you leave the room, the power is deactivated.

Please remember that Italy uses a higher power voltage (220 volts) than North America (110 volts) and differently shaped electrical sockets. Therefore you should pack a plug adaptor for any electric devices.

Fa troppo caldo/freddo nella stanza. Fah TROP-po CAHL-doh/FRED-doh NEL-lah STAHN-zah	It is too hot/cold in the room.
Manca la corrente. MAHN-cah lah cor-REHN-teh	There is no power.
Per favore, potrebbe mettermi in un'altra camera? Pair fah-VO-reh po-TREB-beh MET-tair-mee een oon-AHL-trah CAH-meh-rah	Could you please move me to another room?

Non riesco a capire come funziona la doccia. *(Nohn ree-EHS-co ah cah-PEE-reh CO-meh foon-tsee-OH-nah lah DOHT-chah):* I do not know how the shower operates.

At times, showers or flushing systems in Europe are not very intuitive or are completely different from what you may be accustomed to. The following sentence will help you get some assistance:

Ho problemi con il bagno/ la doccia/il lavandino.
O pro-BLEH-mee kohn eel BAHN-yo/ lah DOHT-chah/eel lah-vahn-DEE-no

I have problems with the toilet/ shower/sink.

 A che ora è il check-out? *(Ah keh OH-rah eh eel check-out):* At what time is checkout?

Checkout times vary; the most common time to check out is 11:00 A.M. Almost all hotels allow the use of their luggage storage room after checking out. This is a good option if you want to spend the day after checking out visiting the city. You can then pick up your luggage and travel to the airport/train station afterward.

Posso lasciare le valige in deposito dopo il check-out?
POS-so lah-SHAH-reh leh vah-LEE-jeh een deh-PO-zee-toh DOH-po eel check-out

Could I leave my luggage in the luggage storage room after checking out?

A che ora parte la navetta/il pulmino per l'aeroporto?
(Ah keh OH-rah PAHR-teh lah nah-VET-tah/il pool-MEE-no pair eel-POR-toh): At what time does the shuttle/minibus leave for the airport?

Most hotels also offer transportation to and from the airport, but it is important to reserve a place to avoid unpleasant surprises. If you prefer to transfer to the airport by taxi, be sure to call ahead for the cab. Public transportation is also a good alternative to reach the airport as the service is often frequent and rather inexpensive; for example, in Rome there is a train every half hour, to and from the Fiumicino Airport.

Per favore, potrebbe prenotarmi un tassì per le otto domani mattina?
Pair fah-VO-reh po-TREB-beh preh-no-TAHR-mee oon tahs-SEE pair leh OT-to doh-MAH-ni maht-TEE-nah

Could you please reserve a taxi for me for eight o'clock tomorrow morning?

Ci sono dei mezzi pubblici per l'aeroporto?
CHEEH SO-no day METS-tsee POOB-blee-chee pair lah-eh-roh-POR-toh

Is there any public transit to the airport?

Chapter 5

Public Transportation

Scusi, dov'è la stazione del treno? *(SCOO-zee doh-VEH lah stah-tsee-OH-neh del TREH-no):* Pardon me, where is the train station?

If you go to Italy either for work or for vacation, you might find yourself in need of a train or a bus. Unlike many North Americans, Italians are used to using public transportation on a daily basis, even if the service is not always great. And since gasoline is so expensive and public transportation is quite affordable in comparison, in most cases taking the train or the bus is the best solution. The only thing you may need is a little patience.

If you must use the train, look for the *stazione ferroviaria* (train station). The *ferrovia* (railway) is well distributed throughout the country, and by train you can reach even secluded locations. Nowadays the system is undergoing some major changes and some train stations are closing. These stations will no longer offer ticketing and information services, but they will keep their stop. This means that even if a train station is closed, there will still be trains stopping there—however, perhaps on a less frequent basis.

Scusi, c'è un bar in questa stazione?	Pardon me, is there a bar in this train station?
SCOO-zee cheh oon bahr een QUEH-stah stah-tsee-OH-neh	
Avrei bisogno di lasciare i miei bagagli in stazione. Come devo fare?	I'd need to leave my luggage in the station. What should I do?
Ah-VRAY bee-ZON-yo dee lah-SHAH-reh ee mee-AY bah-GAHL-yi een stah-tsee-OH-neh CO-meh DEH-vo FAH-reh	
È aperta la biglietteria?	Is the ticket office open?
Eh ah-PAIR-tah lah beel-yet-tair-REE-ah	
Dove sono gli orari dei treni?	Where are the train schedules?
DOH-veh SO-no lyee oh-RAH-ree day TREH-nee	

 Un biglietto di andata e ritorno per Roma Termini, per favore. *(Oon beel-YET-toh dee ahn-DAH-tah eh ree-TOR-no pair RO-ma TAIR-mee-nee pair fah-VO-reh):* A return ticket to Roma Termini, please.

In order to buy a train ticket, you must go to the *biglietteria* (ticket office) inside the train station. If you need information before purchasing your ticket, you must first go to the *ufficio informazioni* (information office). In small train stations, the ticket office takes care of both tasks, but in larger stations the ticket office and the information office are clearly separated—be sure of where to go first to avoid waiting in a long line for nothing. If the ticket office is closed, buy your ticket at the *biglietterie automatiche* (automatic ticket machines) which can be found in every train station. Train tickets can also be bought at some *tabaccai* (tobacco shops) or *giornalai* (newsagents) and online on the Trenitalia website (www.trenitalia.com), which has an English link.

When purchasing your ticket, you must specify your *destinazione* (destination), whether you want a *biglietto di sola andata* (one-way ticket) or a *biglietto di andata e ritorno* (round-trip ticket), and the type of train you want to travel on. Trains can be *regionali* (regional trains), Intercity (long-distance trains), and Eurostar (high-speed long-distance trains). On regional trains there is only one seating class, while on Intercity and Eurostar trains there are *prima* and *seconda classe* (first and second classes).

Scusi, dov'è la sala d'aspetto?	Pardon me, where is the waiting
SCOO-zee doh-VEH lah SAH-lah dah-SPET-toh	room?
A che ora parte il prossimo Intercity per Milano?	What time does the next Intercity train to Milan leave?
Ah keh OH-rah PAHR-teh eel PROS-see-mo Intercity pair Mee-LAH-no	
A che ora arriva questo treno a Genova?	What time does this train arrive in Genoa?
Ah keh OH-rah ahr-REE-vah QUEH-sto TREH-no ah JEHN-oh-vah	

Scusi, dov'è l'obliteratrice? *(SCOO-zee doh-VEH lo-blee-tair-ah-TREE-cheh):* Pardon me, where is the ticket-validating machine?

The most important thing to do before getting on the train is *obliterare il biglietto* (to validate your ticket), which means looking for small yellow machines which are usually located in the train station main hall and validating your ticket there. These machines cannot be found on the *binari* (train platforms), so make sure you find them before looking for your platform. You must validate your ticket before boarding, because the *controllore* (train officer) will surely check your ticket while en route, and if your ticket is not validated, you'll get a fine. Train tickets have a limited *validità* (validity), which depends on the train type, so make sure to check your ticket for that. It is also important to know that unused and unstamped tickets can be refunded at the ticket office.

Scusi, dov'è la carrozza 8?
SCOO-zee doh-VEH lah cahr-ROTS-sah OT-to

Pardon me, where is the car number 8?

Scusi, quello è il mio posto. È prenotato.
SCOO-zee QUEL-lo eh eel MEE-oh PO-sto Eh preh-no-TAH-toh

Pardon me, that is my seat. It is reserved.

Non ha obliterato il biglietto.
Nohn ah oh-blee-tair-AH-toh eel beel-YET-toh

You didn't validate your ticket.

Che differenza di prezzo c'è tra prima e seconda classe?
(Keh deef-fair-EHNT-sah dee PRETS-so cheh trah PREE-mah eh seh-KOHN-dah CLAHS-seh): What price difference is there between first and second class?

Trains differ greatly in terms of quality and services offered. Regional trains are the least expensive but do not offer any services. For example, on a regional train you will not find a *carrozza ristorante* (restaurant car), a *carrozza letto* (sleeping car), or onboard catering. Sometimes you may even have to be prepared for a lack of *aria condizionata* (air-conditioning) in summer or *riscaldamento* (heating) in winter. Regional trains are also slower than other trains as they stop in every city, but quite often they are the only way to reach certain destinations. Intercity and Eurostar trains are more expensive but offer a better service. They are much faster than regional trains, because they only stop in major cities. In terms of services offered, they have bigger seats, catering on board, air-conditioning and heating, and *posti prenotati* (reserved seats).

Remember that Trenitalia, Italy's national train company, is undergoing some major changes, so be prepared for some *ritardi* (delays) while traveling.

C'è una carrozza ristorante su questo treno?	Is there a restaurant car on this train?
Cheh OO-nah cahr-ROTS-sah ree-sto-RAHN-teh soo QUEH-sto TREH-no	
C'è una carrozza letto su questo treno?	Is there a sleeping car on this train?
Cheh OO-nah cahr-ROTS-sah LET-toh soo QUEH-sto TREH-no	
Il treno è in ritardo?	Is the train running late?
Eel TREH-no eh een ree-TAR-doh	

Il volo è in orario? *(Eel VO-loh eh een oh-RAH-ree-oh):* Is the flight on time?

Airports and flights in Italy work exactly the same as everywhere else in the world, so if you are acquainted with all standard air travel procedures, you will know what to expect. Nowadays Alitalia, Italy's national airline, is experiencing a difficult period, so it is common to experience *ritardi* (delays) and *scioperi* (strikes). Italians previously used air travel to go abroad and relied on the train for internal transports, mostly because internal flight fares were much higher than the cost of a train ticket. Today, however, because of budget airlines, it is very common for Italians to use air travel for internal transports, too.

Every major city in Italy has one *aeroporto* (airport), while Rome and Milan have two. The airports are quite far from the city's downtown areas. They can easily be reached *in taxi* (by taxi), *in autobus* (by bus), *in treno* (by train), or sometimes even *in metropolitana* (by subway). Once at the airport, look either for the *arrivi* (arrivals) or *partenze* (departures), depending on your needs. If you are departing, you must *fare il check-in* (check in), *passare i controlli* (go through security controls), and then simply wait at the *porta d'imbarco* (gate) for your *aereo* (plane) to leave. If you are just arriving, after passing though *controllo passaporti* (immigration and passport control) and *dogana* (customs), look for the *ritiro bagagli* (luggage claim) area and then look for the exit. If you are waiting for someone at the airport, go to the arrivals area and check if the flight is *in orario* (on time), *in ritardo* (delayed), or *cancellato* (cancelled).

Scusi, ho perso il volo Alitalia per Milano. Quand'è il prossimo?
Pardon me, I missed the Alitalia flight to Milan. When is the next one?

SCOO-zee oh PAIR-so eel VO-lo
Ahl-ee-TAH-lee-ah pair Mee-LAH-no
QUAHN-deh eel PROS-see-mo

Ho una coincidenza per Napoli. Dove devo andare?
I have a connecting flight for Naples. Where must I go?

Oh oo-nah coh-in-chee-DEHNT-sah
pair NAH-poh-lee DOH-veh
DEH-vo ahn-DAH-reh

Si informano i signori passeggeri che il volo è stato cancellato.
We inform passengers that the flight has been canceled.

See een-FOR-mah-no ee seen-YOR-ee
pahs-sed-JAIR-ee keh eel VO-lo
eh STAH-toh cahn-chel-LAH-toh

 Posso portare questo liquido con me? *(POS-so por-TAH-reh QUEH-sto LEE-quee-do kohn meh):* Can I carry this liquid on board with me?

When it comes to customs, all countries have more or less the same regulations. For international flights, generally passengers are allowed to check two bags of about 50 pounds each. Airlines place their own limits on the number, the size, and the weight of what can be carried onto a flight.

Il mio bagaglio è stato smarrito.   My baggage has gotten lost. Can you
  Mi può aiutare?   help me?
Eel MEE-oh bah-GAHL-yo eh STAH-toh
    smahr-REE-toh Mee poo-OH
    aye-oo-TAH-reh

 Scusi, è questo l'autobus per l'aeroporto? *(SCOO-zee eh QUEH-sto LAH-oo-toh-boos pair lah-eh-roh-POR-toh):* Pardon me, is this the bus for the airport?

Every Italian city has a good public transportation system consisting of *autobus* (buses), which either run *in centro* (within the city center) or connect the center with *la periferia* (the suburbs). There are also buses that run between cities, which are normally called *pullman* or *corriera* and are bigger and more comfortable than the city buses.

You can buy tickets for the buses at a *tabaccaio* (tobacco shop), at a *giornalaio* (newsagent), at tourist information offices, sometimes in train stations, and surely at the *sede centrale* (main office) of each bus company. Only in a very few cases can you buy your tickets on board, so make sure you have your ticket before getting on the bus. Finding a *cartina* or *mappa* (transit system map) can be a bit difficult; if you need one ask the tourist information office or the bus company's main office.

Once on board, you must validate your ticket. This is important, because you will be fined if your ticket is checked and found not validated. In most cases, you do not need a transfer, as your ticket is valid for unlimited travel for a certain amount of time. If you are transferring from one bus to another, simply carry your ticket with you without validating it another time. Since the system can change slightly from city to city, if unsure, it is always better to ask if a transfer is needed while buying the ticket. In just a few cities you can find *tram* (street-cars), too, but they are part of the city bus system, so everything operates the same.

Whatever information you may need while on board, you may ask the *autista* (driver) or your fellow passengers.

Ferma qui il bus per la stazione? Does the bus to the station stop here?
FAIR-mah kwee eel boos pair lah
   stah-tsee-OH-neh

Quante fermate ci sono prima di How many stops are there before
   arrivare al Colosseo? getting to the Coliseum?
QUAHN-teh fair-MAH-teh chee SO-no
   PREE-mah dee ahr-ree-VAH-reh
   ahl Co-los-SEH-oh

Scusi, qual è la prossima fermata? Sorry, what is the next stop?
SCOO-zee quahl eh lah PROS-see-
   mah fair-MAH-tah

Dove devo scendere per andare Where must I get off to go
   in centro? downtown?
DOH-veh DEH-vo SHEHN-deh-reh
   pair ahn-DAH-reh een CHEHN-tro

 Un biglietto per la metropolitana, per favore. *(Oon beel-YET-toh pair lah meh-tro-po-lee-TAH-nah pair fah-VO-reh):* A ticket for the subway, please.

Today, only a few cities in Italy have a *metropolitana* (subway system): Milan, Rome, Naples, Turin, Genoa, Palermo, Catania, and Cagliari. In most cases it is a very small system, consisting of only a few lines. The biggest system is the one in Milan, where currently there are three lines and another three are under construction.

The metro or subway system works more or less the same as that of buses. Tickets are purchased at a *tabaccaio* (tobacco shop), at a *giornalaio* (newsagent), or at the *sportelli* (ticket counters) in each *stazione della metropolitana* (metro station), or from *biglietterie automatiche* (automatic ticket machines) if the counters are closed. Usually a ticket is valid only for one trip; therefore it does not have a specific time validity. In most cases, one ticket costs about one euro, and you can buy *biglietti giornalieri* (daily tickets), *biglietti settimanali* (weekly tickets), and *biglietti mensili* (monthly tickets), or buy a *carnet*, which offers a certain number of tickets at a discounted price. Sometimes there are also tourist passes, so check with the tourist office or the ticket counter for information. In a few cases, you can use your bus ticket for the subway, too, but since every system is different, make sure it is allowed before relying on that. For subway hours of operation, check with either the tourist office or the subway ticket counter as well.

Vorrei un carnet da dieci biglietti. I'd like to have a ten-ticket book.
Vor-RAY oon car-NEH da dee-EH-
    chee beel-YET-tee

Quanto costa il biglietto How much is the daily ticket?
giornaliero?
QUAHN-toh CO-stah eel beel-YET-toh
    jor-nah-lee-EH-ro

Posso usare il biglietto del bus per la metropolitana?
Can I use the bus ticket for the subway?

POS-so oo-ZAH-reh eel beel-YET-toh del boos pair lah meh-tro-po-lee-TAH-nah

Potrebbe darmi una cartina della metropolitana?
Could you give me a subway system map?

Po-TREB-beh DAHR-mee OO-nah cahr-TEE-nah DEL-lah meh-tro-po-lee-TAH-nah

 Mi potrebbe chiamare un taxi, per piacere? *(Mee po-TREB-beh kee-ah-MAH-reh oon TAH-xee pair peeah-CHEH-reh)*: Could you call a taxi for me, please?

Even if Italian cities have a good public transportation system, a taxi is sometimes needed, perhaps late at night, or when you need to go to the airport and do not want to carry heavy suitcases, or simply to go somewhere quickly. In a hotel or restaurant, it is easier to have someone call a taxi for you; however, at the airport or train station, you must *mettersi in coda* (get in line) at the *fermata dei taxi* (taxi stand) just outside the main exit. Regardless of how you are traveling, upon arrival in a new city be sure to have the number of a taxi agency handy in case of need.

Once in the taxicab, make sure the *tassista* (taxi driver) understands where you need to go, and, most importantly, make sure you know in advance how much you are expected to pay for the *corsa* (ride). If you are unsure about the *cifra* (amount of money), don't be shy; ask that the driver *scriverlo su un pezzo di carta* (write it on a piece of paper). Tourists are common prey all over the world and Italy is no exception.

Dovrei andare all'albergo Miramare. Do-VRAY ahn-DAH-reh ahl-lahl-BEHR-go Mee-rah-MAH-reh	I need to go to the Miramare Hotel.
Quanto costa la corsa per l'aeroporto? QUAHN-toh CO-stah lah COR-sah pair lah-eh-roh-POR-toh	How much is the ride to the airport?
Quanto ci vuole per arrivare in centro? QUAHN-toh chee voo-OH-leh pair ahr-ree-VAH-reh een CHEHN-tro	How much does it take to get to the city center?
Potrebbe mandare un taxi al ristorante Margherita? Po-TREB-beh mahn-DAH-reh oon TAH-xee ahl ree-sto-RAHN-teh Mahr-geh-REE-tah	Can you send a taxi to the Margherita restaurant?

 Vorrei affittare una bicicletta. (*Vor-RAY ahf-feet-TAH-reh OO-nah bee-chee-CLET-tah*): I'd like to rent a bike.

Bikes can be rented only in very few cities in Italy. In some areas of Italy, like the Pianura Padana, where the land is flat, *biciclette* (bikes) are widely used as a means of transportation, while in the rest of Italy using a bike to go to work or to go to the city center can be difficult, if not dangerous. Most cities have only a few cycle tracks, and cycling in the city traffic can be a very unpleasant experience. Therefore, finding a bike to rent may not be easy, unless you are in a tourist area.

Bringing your own bike to Italy can be quite challenging as well. However, on certain trains bikes are allowed on board with you, so this could be an interesting and different way of touring Italy. If you are really brave, consider renting a *motorino* (scooter), but be prepared to face the crazy city drivers.

Ci sono piste ciclabili in questa città?
Chee SO-no PEE-steh chee-CLAH-bee-lee een QUEH-stah cheet-TAH

Are there cycle tracks in this city?

Posso salire sul treno con la bicicletta?
POS-so sah-LEE-reh sool TREH-no kohn lah bee-chee-CLET-tah

Can I get on the train with the bike?

Scusi, quanto costa affittare un motorino?
SCOO-zee QUAHN-toh CO-stah ahf-feet-TAH-reh oon mo-to-REE-no

Pardon me, how much is it to rent a scooter?

Chapter 6

Driving

Vorrei affittare una macchina sportiva. *(Vor-RAY ahf-feet-TAH-reh OO-nah MAHK-kee-nah spor-TEE-vah):* I'd like to rent a sports car.

Italy has so many lovely hidden spots to visit that it can be fun to rent a car to drive around freely and make the most of your time. You can find *compagnie di autonoleggio* (car rental agencies) in every airport or in main train stations. The most common rental agencies are Avis, Hertz, Budget, Europcar, Maggiore, and Sixt. Car rental works exactly as it does in North America; you can *prenotare online* (reserve online) if you like, and you can *ritirare* (pick up) your car in one place and *riconsegnare* (return) it in another. You must pay *con carta di credito* (with credit card) and have a *patente di guida valida* (valid driver's licence) and *un documento d'identità* (a piece of identification) in order to rent a car.

When renting a car, there is a large choice of vehicles to choose from: an *auto piccola* or *economica* (small car) like a Fiat Panda or a Fiat Punto; an *auto di medie dimensioni* (medium-size car) like a Volkswagen Golf; or an *auto di grandi dimensioni* (large car) like big Audis or Volkswagens. Apart from the rental agency auto classification, in Italy cars are normally divided into *utilitarie* (economy cars), *berline* (sedans), station wagons, SUVs, *fuoristrada* (off-road vehicles), and *sportive* (sports cars). Most people in Italy buy small cars, because streets are narrow and even parking spots are quite tiny.

Quanto costa affittare una macchina per una settimana?	How much is it to rent a car for one week?
QUAHN-toh CO-stah ahf-feet-TAH-reh OO-nah MAHK-kee-nah pair OO-nah set-tee-MAH-nah	
Posso riconsegnare la macchina a Roma?	Can I return the car in Rome?
POS-so ree-kohn-sehn-YAH-reh lah MAHK-kee-nah ah RO-mah	
Che tipi di veicoli avete?	What kinds of cars do you have?
Keh TEE-pee dee veh-EE-co-lee ah-VEH-teh	
Potrei avere una macchina più grande/più piccola?	Could I have a bigger/smaller car?
Po-TRAY ah-VEH-reh OO-nah MAHK-kee-nah PEW GRAHN-deh/PEW PEEK-ko-lah	

 Vorrei una macchina con il cambio automatico. *(Vohr-RAY OO-nah MAHK-kee-nah kohn eel CAHM-bee-oh ah-oo-toh-MAH-tee-co):* I'd like a car with automatic transmission.

Normally cars have *cambio manuale* (standard transmission), but cars with *cambio automatico* (automatic drive) are available if you ask well in advance. You may want to ask for *condizionatore* or *aria condizionata* (air conditioner or air-conditioning), *chiusura centralizzata* (central locking), and *alzacristalli elettrici* (electric windows). In terms of fuel, choose between a *motore a benzina* (gas-powered engine) and a *motore diesel* (diesel-powered engine). Cars with a diesel-powered engine usually need less fuel and therefore are more economical than those running on gasoline.

La macchina ha il navigatore satellitare?

Does the car have GPS?

Lah MAHK-kee-nah ah eel nah-vee-gah-TOH-reh sah-tehl-lee-TAH-reh

 Quanto è il limite di velocità nei centri abitati? *(QUAHN-toh EH eel LEE-mee-teh-dee veh-loh-chee-TAH neh-ee CHEN-tree ah-bee-TAH-tee):* What is the speed limit in the city streets?

When driving in Italy or in any other country, make sure to familiarize yourself with the traffic laws. For example, in Italy it is against the law to make a right turn on a red light; on a multiple lane highway it is not allowed to overtake another car by passing on the right. Furthermore, you must adapt to the position and height of traffic lights; at times the *rotonde* (circles or roundabouts) can be a bit confusing; and of course, drivers face traffic jams in many Italian cities.

Si può andare in macchina al centro storico?

Are you permitted to drive your car in the historical center of town?

See PWO ahn-DAH-reh in MAHK-kee-nah al CHEN-troh STOH-ree-coh

Corso Italia è un'isola pedonale.   Corso Italia is a pedestrian-only zone.

KOR-soh ee-TAH-lee-ah EH oon

  EE-soh-la peh-doh-NAH-leh

 Scusi, dov'è l'entrata dell'autostrada? *(SCOO-zee doh-VEH lehn-TRAH-tah del-lah-oo-toh-STRAH-dah):* Pardon me, where is the toll road entrance?

After renting a car, start driving and having some fun on the Italian roads. Be cautious, however, as Italian drivers are considered very wild!

Roads in Italy are classified as *strade statali, provinciali o comunali,* which are just standard roads pertaining either to the state, the province, or the city. Then there are the *superstrade* (highways), which are faster roads outside the city center, and *tangenziali* (ring roads or beltways), which run around the center of a big city. The *autostrade* (toll roads) are fast highways that take you everywhere in Italy, but that request the payment of a ticket. On entering the *autostrada,* you must stop and take a *biglietto* (ticket), which you hand in when exiting, at which time you will also pay the necessary fee. The *pedaggio* (toll road ticket) can be paid in cash or with credit card; just make sure to choose the corresponding lane upon exiting. Cash lanes have a sign displaying coins; the others a sign displaying cards. Some lanes have employees handling your payment; others have automatic machines. If your car has a *Telepass* (a small machine that handles automatic exit and payment), simply look for the *Telepass* lanes and drive through: the owner of the car will be charged afterward on his or her bank account.

If you ask for directions and distances, remember that distances in Italy are measured by the kilometer, which corresponds to 0.62 miles.

Posso avere la ricevuta del pagamento?	Can I have the receipt?
POS-so ah-VEH-reh lah ree-ceh-VOO-tah del pah-gah-MEHN-toh	
Ho perso il mio biglietto. Cosa devo fare?	I have lost my ticket. What should I do?
Oh PAIR-so eel MEE-oh beel-YET-toh CO-sah DEH-vo FAH-reh	
Ho sbagliato uscita. Posso rientrare in autostrada?	I have taken the wrong exit. Can I enter the toll road again?
Oh sbahl-YAH-toh oo-SHEE-tah POS-so ree-ehn-TRA-reh een ah-oo-toh-STRAH-da	
Quanti chilometri ci sono per arrivare in città?	How many kilometers are there to get to the city?
QUAHN-tee kee-LO-meh-tree chee SO-no pair ahr-ree-VAH-reh een cheet-TAH	

 Favorisca patente e libretto di circolazione. *(Fah-vo-REE-scah pah-TEHN-teh eh lee-BRET-toh dee cheer-co-lah-tsee-OH-neh)*: Driver's licence and logbook, please.

Limiti di velocità (speed limits) on the *autostrade* vary from 80 kilometers per hour (50 miles per hour) to a maximum of 130 km/h (80 mph); however, on *superstrade* limits can be between 50 km/h (30 mph) and

110 km/h (70 mph). In cities the speed limit is 50 km/h. Use caution when driving; *multe per limiti di velocità* (fines for speeding tickets) can be very high. Remember also that in Italy it is mandatory to wear *cinture di sicurezza* (seat belts), it is forbidden to use mobile phones when driving, and there are huge fines and criminal charges for *guida in stato di ubriachezza* (DUI).

Controlli stradali (road controls) can be handled by different corps: *polizia stradale* (highway police), *Carabinieri* (a different force which is part of the Italian army and deals with security-keeping tasks), *polizia provinciale* (county police), and *vigili urbani* (metropolitan police). Officers can pull a car over, even if the driver didn't do anything wrong, just to ask for a *controllo* (check). In that case, you'll be asked to show your *patente* (driver's license) and *libretto* (vehicle registration certificate), and they may check your *bollo d'assicurazione* (insurance stamp), which has to be clearly exposed on the windshield.

Ha superato i limiti di velocità e devo farle la multa.	You have exceeded the speed limit and I have to give you a ticket.
Ah soo-pair-AH-toh ee LEE-mee-tee dee veh-lo-chee-TAH eh DEH-vo FAHR-leh lah MOOL-tah	
Come mai guidava così veloce?	Why were you driving so fast?
CO-meh my gwi-DAH-vah co-ZEE veh-LO-cheh	
Potrei vedere il suo certificato di assicurazione?	May I see your insurance documents?
Po-TRAY veh-DEH-reh eel SOO-oh chair-tee-fee-CAH-toh dee ahs-see-coo-rah-tsee-OH-neh	

È una macchina in affitto? Is it a rental car?
Eh OO-nah MAHK-kee-nah een
   ahf-FEET-oh

 Vorrei fare il pieno di benzina verde. *(Vor-RAY FAH-reh eel pee-EH-no dee behn-TSEE-nah VAIR-deh):* I'd like to fill up the tank with unleaded gasoline.

Stazioni di servizio or *benzinai* (gas stations) can be found everywhere in Italy: in the city center or on main highways and of course on the *autostrade* (toll roads). The most common names are Agip, Esso, Ip, Q8, Api, Erg, Shell, and Tamoil. The big gas stations on highways usually have a bar and a small shop, while those on the *autostrade* may even have a snack bar, a restaurant, and a small grocery store. These stations are called *autogrill*. In most gas stations, big or small, there will be a car wash, and you can also find oil-change and tire-inflation services.

In terms of fuel, you can choose between *benzina verde* (unleaded gas) and *diesel* or *gasolio* (diesel), depending on the engine of your car. Fuel is much more expensive in Italy than in North America. In the past, diesel was much less expensive than gas, but today the two cost roughly the same. Gas stations usually have *benzinai* (attendants) who take care of filling up tanks during the day (mostly from 8 A.M. to 8 P.M.), while in the evening or on weekends it is self-service. In large gas stations, however, it is permissible to fill up the tank by yourself, even when attendants are in service, to get a discount. At gas stations you can pay either in cash or with credit cards.

Quanto dista il prossimo autogrill? How far is the next *autogrill*?
QUAHN-toh DEE-stah eel
   PROS-see-mo ah-oo-toh-GREEL

C'è un autolavaggio in questa Is there a car wash in this gas station?
  stazione di servizio?
Cheh oon ah-oo-toh-lah-VAHD-jo
   een QUEH-stah stah-tsee-OH-neh
   dee sair-VEET-see-oh

Dieci euro di diesel, per favore. Ten euros of diesel, please.
Dee-EH-chee eh-OO-ro dee
   DEE-zel pair fah-VO-reh

C'è lo sconto self-service? Is there a discount for self-service?
Cheh lo SCON-toh self-service

 È possibile guidare la macchina in centro? *(Eh poh-SEE-bee-leh gwi-DAH-reh een CHEHN-troh):* Are cars allowed downtown?

In some cities, the historic center of town is off-limits to cars. In these cases, park your car in a public lot and visit the town on foot.

Dove posso parcheggiare Where can I park my car?
  la macchina?
DOh-veh POS-soh pahr-keh-JAH-reh
   lah MAHK-kee-nah

Potrebbe fare un controllo generale alla macchina?

(Po-TREB-beh FAH-reh oon kohn-TROL-lo jeh-neh-RAH-leh AHL-lah MAHK-kee-nah): Can you do a general check on my car?

If your car has a problem, look for a *meccanico* (garage). Garages can be found in every city and they are usually open from Monday through Friday from 8 A.M. to 1 P.M. and then again from 3 P.M. to 7 P.M. Some of them may be open on Saturday also, but all of them are surely closed on Sunday and for festivities. There are small garages on the *autostrada*, as well; usually each *autogrill* has one.

Garages generally take care of problems related to a car's engine, so if you need some fixing to its body look for a *carrozzeria* (body shop), and for specific problems with lights and the electrical system see an *elettrauto* (electric garage). In most cases, though, large garages can handle all issues without problems. If there is no specific problem, but you just want a checkup, ask them for a general check or an oil change or some tire inflation, too.

Il faro sinistro posteriore della macchina non funziona. Potrebbe cambiare la lampadina, per favore?

The left rear light of my car is not working. Could you please change the lamp?

Eel FAH-ro see-NEE-stro po-steh-ree-OH-reh DEL-lah MAHK-kee-nah nohn foon-tsee-OH-nah Po-TREB-beh cahm-bee-AH-reh lah lahm-pah-DEE-nah pair fah-VO-reh

Potrebbe dare un'occhiata alle gomme? Mi sembrano un po' sgonfie.
Po-TREB-beh DAH-reh oon-ok-kee-AH-tah AHL-leh GOM-meh Mee SEHM-brah-no oon po SGON-fee-eh

Can you check the tires? It seems as if they are a bit flat.

Avrei bisogno del cambio d'olio.
Ah-VRAY bee-ZON-yo del CAHM-bee-oh DO-lee-oh

I need an oil change.

La macchina fa uno strano rumore. Può controllare?
Lah MAHK-kee-nah fah OO-no STRAH-no roo-MO-reh Poo-OH kohn-trol-LAH-reh

The car makes a strange noise. Can you check it?

 Potrebbe suggerire una strada con veduta scenica?
(Poh-TREB-beh su-jeh-REE-reh OO-na STRAH-dah kohn veh-DOO-tah SHAY-nee-kah): Can you suggest a scenic driving route?

Italy is famous for its beautiful, scenic driving tours. Before going on a driving trip, however, it's best to know the distances involved in order to budget for gas and travel time. Planning ahead is especially important if you are renting a car.

Quanto dista Pisa da Firenze?
QUAHN-toh DEE-stah PEE-zah dah Fee-rehn-zeh

How far is it from Pisa to Florence?

Chapter 7

Shopping

 Dove posso trovare un negozio di vestiti? *(DO-veh POS-so tro-VAH-reh oon neh-GOH-tsee-oh dee veh-STEE-tee):* Where can I find a clothing store?

In Italian the expression *fare shopping* is widely used and it normally means to go shopping for clothes. Fashion in Italy is a very important business and all over the world Italy is known for fashion brands like Prada, Armani, Gucci, and Versace, which are the most expensive and exclusive ones, but also for other less upscale names like Benetton. Italy is most often associated with style and fashion and many Italians take pride in always being *ben vestiti* (well dressed) and in keeping with the latest *tendenze* (trends). Young Italians want to be *alla moda* (hip with the latest trends) and in most cases would never wear something that is *fuori moda* (out of style). The most important city in Italy in terms of fashion is Milan, where you can find the headquarters of all the *marche di vestiti* (clothing brands). It is a paradise for shoppers; there are stores to satisfy every need.

Fare shopping is something that is normally done on Saturday afternoons, when the main streets of even the smallest towns are full of people who shop for clothes or simply take a peek at the *vetrine* (store windows).

In most cases, the exclusive shops and the boutiques are located in the downtown area of each town, which in Italy is normally the *centro storico* (historical center). Shops are lined along the streets and usually each town has at least one famous street where shoppers go to look for real Italian-style shopping. In most cases, shops and *boutiques* (elegant shops) are open from Monday through Saturday, from 9 A.M. to 1 P.M. and then again from 4 P.M. to 8 P.M. In large cities or in tourist areas it is more common to find shops which are open all day, mostly from 9 A.M. to 8 P.M. All stores are normally closed on Sunday, except during the Christmas period.

C'è un grande magazzino qui vicino?	Is there a department store nearby?
Cheh oon GRAHN-deh mah-gaht-TSEE-no kwee vee-CHEE-no	
Scusi, dov'è il centro commerciale?	Pardon me, where is the shopping mall?
SCOO-zee doh-VEH eel CHEHN-tro cohm-mair-CHAH-leh	
Scusi, è questa la strada per l'outlet?	Pardon me, is this the road to the outlet center?
SCOO-zee eh QUEH-stah lah STRAH-dah pair lah outlet	
Scusi, sa a che ora chiudono i negozi?	Pardon me, do you know when the shops close?
SCOO-zee sah ah keh OH-rah kee-OO-doh-no ee neh-GOH-tsee	

Dove trovo una piantina del centro commerciale?

(DO-veh TRO-vo OO-nah pee-an-TEE-nah del CHEHN-tro cohm-mair-CHAH-leh): Where can I find a map of the shopping mall?

Centri commerciali (shopping malls) have become very popular in Italy in the last ten to fifteen years, and, even though it is more common to go there to shop for food or for electronics, people love to buy clothes there, too. In most shopping malls, however, there are only *grandi catene* (chain stores) and less exclusive fashion brands. Just as in North America, shopping malls in Italy are large places where you can find every kind of shop: *negozi di vestiti* (clothing stores), *scarpe* (shoes), *elettrodomestici* (home appliances), *telefoni cellulari* (mobile phones), *mobili* (furniture), *giocattoli* (toys), and also some cafeterias and fast food. They are usually outside urban areas and sometimes just outside the city center. Normally malls are open from 9 A.M. to 9 P.M. every day of the week, Sunday included. Large shopping malls close only on national holidays in Italy.

Dov'è l'ascensore?	Where is the elevator?
Do-VEH lah-shehn-SO-reh	
Come arrivo al parcheggio?	How do I get to the parking lot?
CO-meh ahr-REE-vo ahl pahr-KED-jo	
Dov'è il bancomat?	Where is the ATM?
Do-VEH eel BAHN-co-maht	
Scusi, dov'è l'uscita più vicina?	Pardon me, where is the nearest exit?
SCOO-zee doh-VEH loo-SHEE-tah PEW vee-CHEE-nah	

Dov'è il reparto donna? *(Doh-VEH eel reh-PAHR-toh DON-nah):* Where is the women's department?

In Italy *grandi magazzini* (department stores) can be found only in the largest cities like Milan, Rome, Turin, and a few others. The oldest and most upscale department store in Italy is La Rinascente, where you can find all the most well-known fashion brands, including the most expensive ones. Other department stores are Coin and Upim, which are a bit less expensive and exclusive than La Rinascente.

Just like in North America, department stores have different *reparti* (departments), and they usually sell *vestiti da uomo* (men's clothing), *vestiti da donna* (women's clothing), *vestiti da bambino* (children's clothing), *borse* (bags), *scarpe* (shoes), *accessori* (accessories), *biancheria intima* (lingerie), *profumi* (perfumes), *accessori regalo* (gifts), and *accessori per la casa* (home accessories). Some of them also have a *reparto gioielleria* (jewelry department), where you can find *anelli* (rings), *collane* (necklaces), *orecchini* (earrings), and *orologi* (watches). In a few trendy department stores, like Coin or La Rinascente, there are also gourmet foods, where the most exquisite products from Italy and other parts of the world are sold. In most department stores you can also find a nice café or a small restaurant inside, where shoppers can relax and rest from a busy shopping day. These eateries can be very big and divided on different floors and are usually open all day, from 9 A.M. to 8 P.M., sometimes even on Sunday.

Dov'è il reparto uomo?	Where is the men's department?
Do-VEH eel reh-PAHR-toh oo-OH-mo	
Dov'è il reparto calzature?	Where is the shoe department?
Doh-VEH eel reh-PAHR-toh cahl-tsah-TOO-reh	

C'è un ristorante in questo grande Is there a restaurant in this
  magazzino?   department store?
Cheh oon ree-sto-RAHN-teh een
  QUEH-sto GRAHN-deh
  mah-gaht-TSEE-no
Scusi, sa dov'è il reparto Pardon me, do you know where the
  biancheria intima?   lingerie department is?
SCOO-zee sah doh-VEH eel
  reh-PAHR-toh bee-ahn-keh-
  REE-ah EEN-tee-mah

 Quando iniziano i saldi? *(QUAHN-doh ee-NEE-tsee-ah-no ee SAHL-dee):* When do the sales start?

Factory outlet malls (commonly called *outlet* in Italian) are very popular in Italy nowadays, because in these malls there are outlet shops selling designer and premium brands at a discounted price. The first and largest outlet mall in Italy is in Serravalle Scrivia, near Alessandria, in northern Italy. It opened only a few years ago and was an immediate success, which led to other outlets being opened around the country. Today there are at least five or six outlet centers in Italy. Just like shopping malls, they are open all days of the week from 9 A.M. to 9 P.M., and they are usually located far from urban areas but very close to the main *autostrade* (highways). Outlet centers are very popular during *saldi* (sales), when people swarm to them looking for designer brands at an even greater discounted price. Sales do not take place only in outlets but are found in every shop. Basically there are *saldi invernali* (winter sales), which normally start around January 10 and last until mid-February, and *saldi estivi* (summer sales), which start around mid-July and last until the beginning of September. The government of each region decides these dates and each shop must stick to them. Apart from summer and winter sales, there can be other sales called *svendita* or *liquidazione totale*, which can take place when a shop is closing or is going to be renovated. In the larger outlet malls there are good bargains all year round.

Scusi, questo è in saldo?
Pardon me, is this on sale?
SCOO-zee QUEH-sto eh een
SAHL-doh

Quant'è lo sconto?
How much is the discount?
QUAHN-teh lo SCON-toh

È in saldo solo la merce estiva/ invernale?
Are only summer/winter clothes on sale?
Eh een SAHL-doh SO-lo lah
MAIR-cheh eh-STEE-vah/
een-vair-NAH-leh

Ci sono negozi che fanno svendite in questa zona?
Are there shops with sales in this area?
Chee SO-no neh-GOH-tsee keh
FAHN-no SVEN-dee-teh een
QUEH-stah ZO-nah

 Vorrei provare questo vestito. *(Vor-RAY pro-VAH-reh QUEH-sto veh-STEE-toh):* I'd like to try this dress/suit.

In large department stores and shopping malls you are free to enter every shop, just browse, and in most cases help yourself with clothes. If you need help, ask the *commessa* (shop assistant), but usually you are free to choose and try on clothes by yourself. In smaller shops it is more polite to first ask to take a look before browsing in the shop.

In most cases, you'll be allowed to look without being disturbed by either the shop assistant or the shop owner. It is, however, important to keep in mind that you cannot mess up clothes in the shop and just leave.

In a clothing store you can usually find *vestiti da donna* (dresses), *vestiti da uomo* (suits), *pantaloni* (trousers), *gonne* (skirts), *maglie di lana* (wool sweaters), *maglie di cotone* (cotton sweaters), *felpe* (sweat-shirts), *camicie* (shirts), *magliette* (T-shirts), *giubbotti* (jackets), *cappotti* (coats), *sciarpe* (scarves), *cappelli* (hats), *guanti* (hand gloves), and *cravatte* (ties). In a lingerie store, however, you can find *mutande da uomo* (boxer shorts), *mutande da donna* (ladies underwear), *collant* (tights), and *calze* (socks). In terms of materials or fabrics, either look for clothes *di seta* (made of silk), *di lana* (made of wool), *di cotone* (made of cotton), or *acrilici* (acrylic).

Dove sono le cabine di prova?   Where are the fitting rooms?
DOH-veh SO-no leh CAH-bee-neh
   dee PRO-vah

Posso dare un'occhiata?   Can I take a look?
POS-so DAH-reh oon-ok-kee-AH-tah

 Ha questa camicia in blu? *(AH QUEH-stah Kah-MEE-chee-ah in blu):* Do you have this shirt in blue?

For many people, color coordination is important for dressing. Which colors go well together? What color combination should be avoided? Which are the accessories (*accessori*) that need to be coordinated? If color coordination is important for your look (*look*), get some sound advice or a second opinion by asking the salesperson. White (*il bianco*) and black (*il nero*) go well with almost any color. Red (*il rosso*)

goes well (*si abbina*) with colors of the same tonality (*tonalità*) like purple (*il viola*) or pink (*il rosa*); however, it should not be matched with green (*il verde*), yellow (*il giallo*), or blue (*il blu*).

Come mi sta questa gonna rossa con la camicetta bianca?

CO-meh mee stah QUEH-stah GOHN-nah RO-sah kohn lah cah-mee-CHEHT-tah bee-AHN-cah

How does this red skirt look with the white blouse?

Le scarpe e la borsa rosse sono molto chic.

Leh SKAHR-peh eh lah BOHR-sah ROHS-seh SOH-no MOHL-toh sheek

The red shoes and purse are very classy.

I jeans chiari e la maglietta gialla sono molto eleganti.

Ee jeens kee-AH-ree eh lah mahl-YEHT-tah SO-no MOHL-toh eh-leh-GUN-tee

The light-colored jeans and the yellow sweater are very elegant.

Potrei provare una tonalità più scura?

POH-tray proh-VAH-reh OO-na toh-nah-lee-TAH PEW SKUH-rah

Can I try one with a darker shade?

Potrei avere una taglia più grande/più piccola?

(Po-TRAY ah-VEH-reh OO-nah TAHL-yah PEW GRAHN-deh/ PEW PEEK-ko-lah): Can I have a bigger/smaller size?

If you are shopping for clothes in Italy, keep in mind that sizes are different, so make sure you know the right *misura* (measurement). For sweaters and T-shirts, the system is more or less the same as in North America: there are *taglia piccola* (small), *taglia media* (medium), and *taglia forte* (large). Usually you can use the English terms "small," "medium," "large," and "extra large," as well, and you will be perfectly understood. Sizes are exactly the same as in North America for jeans also. Measurements are a little different for dresses, skirts, and trousers, however. The following is a size comparison chart, so that you know what to ask the *commessa* (shop assistant) for. Also keep in mind that there is no difference between *taglie da uomo* (men's sizes) and *taglie da donna* (women's sizes).

Italian	American Women	American Men
42	8	32
44	10	34
46	12	36
48	14	38
50	16	40
52	18	42
54	20	44

Vorrei un paio di pantaloni taglia 44.

I'd like a pair of trousers size 34.

Vor-RAY oon PYE-oh dee pahn-tah-LO-nee TAHL-yah quah-RAHN-tah-QUAT-tro

Vorrei cambiare questo vestito perché non mi va bene.

(Vor-RAY cahm-bee-AH-reh QUEH-sto veh-STEE-toh pair-KEH nohn mee vah BEH-neh): I'd like to exchange this dress/suit because it doesn't fit.

In Italy it is not always easy to return your clothes to the store if you don't like them. Some big chain stores or department stores have a clear return policy which you can easily find on the back of your receipt, but you might want to double-check with small shop owners about their return policy. It may be problematic or they may only allow exchanges within a short period of time. Even if these shop owners will exchange your clothes for other merchandise, it is very unlikely that they will accept your clothes and give you money back (*dare indietro i soldi*). Most of the time, if *clienti* (customers) do not want to exchange clothes for other merchandise, they will be given a *buono* (coupon) for the amount of money they spent, which can be used in the same store within a certain period of time.

Vorrei cambiare questo vestito perché ha un difetto.
Vor-RAY cahm-bee-AH-reh QUEH-sto veh-STEE-toh pair-CHE ah oon dee-FET-toh

I'd like to exchange this dress, because it has a flaw.

Vorrei cambiare questa borsa con un'altra.
Vor-RAY cahm-bee-AH-reh QUEH-stah BOHR-sah kohn oon-AHL-trah

I'd like to exchange this purse with another one.

Potrei avere un buono in cambio?
Po-TRAY ah-VEH-reh oon boo-OH-no een CAHM-bee-oh

May I have a store credit in exchange?

Questa gonna è troppo grande.   This skirt is too big. Can I exchange it?
  Posso cambiarla?
QUEH-stah GOHN-nah eh TROP-po
  GRAHN-deh POS-so cahm-bee-
  AHR-lah

 Avete un paio di stivali numero 38? *(Ah-VEH-teh oon PYE-oh dee stee-VAH-lee NOO-meh-ro trehn-TOT-to):* Do you have a pair of boots size 6½?

Certain areas of Italy, like Tuscany, for example, are renowned for their high-quality leather, and there you can find great bargains on shoes and bags. Almost everywhere, there are good quality accessories at a fair price. If you enter a shoe store looking for women's shoes, you might ask for *scarpe a tacco alto* (high-heeled shoes), *scarpe a tacco basso* (low-heeled shoes), or *scarpe senza tacco* (shoes with no heel). For both men and women you can ask for *mocassini* (mocassins), *scarpe da ginnastica* (sneakers), *infradito* (flip-flops), and *stivali* (boots). If you are looking for *ciabatte* (slippers), you could ask in a shoe store, but it is more common to find them in either a lingerie or clothing store. In terms of shoe brands, there is a big choice: you can either go from the very expensive and stylish brands like Rossetti, Ferragamo, Vicini, or to more affordable but still very trendy brands like Nero Giardini.

Shoe sizes in Italy are different from those in North America. Please see the following chart, so that you know what to ask for. And note that, as with clothing sizes, in Italy there is no difference between men's and women's shoe sizes.

Female (U.S)	Female (Italian)
3½	35
4	35½
4½	36
5	36½
5½	37
6	37½
6½	38
7	38½
7½	39
8	40
8½	41
9	41½
9½	42
10	42½
10½	43

Male (U.S.)	Male (Italian)
5	36½
5½	37
6	37½
6½	38
7	38½
7½	39
8	40
8½	41
9	41½
9½	42
10	42½
10½	43
11	44
11½	44½
12	45
12½	46

Potrei provare quelle scarpe in vetrina?

Po-TRAY pro-VAH-reh QUEHL-leh SCAR-peh een veh-TREE-nah

Can I try those shoes in the window?

Queste scarpe sono piccole. Posso avere una misura più grande?

QUEH-steh SCAR-peh SO-no PEEK-ko-leh POS-so ah-VEH-reh OO-nah mee-ZOO-rah PEW GRAHN-deh

These shoes are small. Can I have a bigger size?

 Avete una borsa di pelle e un portafoglio coordinato?

(Ah-VEH-teh OO-nah BOHR-sah dee PEL-leh eh oon por-tah-FOHL-yo co-or-dee-NAH-toh): Do you have a leather bag and a matching purse?

Regarding *borse* (bags) and other fashionable accessories, Italy has the largest possible selection to choose from. Bags are normally sold in either clothing or shoe stores, and all the well-known fashion brands have their own line of bags, so it is really up to your own personal taste to find the perfect one. The Marche region in Italy is the area where all Italian shoe factories are located, and there you can find the outlets of the most well-known brands—where there are not only shoes and bags but also *portafogli da donna* (purses), *portafogli da uomo* (wallets), *valige* (suitcases), and *cinture* (belts) of the finest quality at a discounted price. If you are lucky, you might even find places to have shoes made in your design and exact foot size.

Potrebbe incartarmi quella Could you wrap that belt please? It
  cintura, per favore? È un regalo. is a gift.
Po-TREB-beh-teh een-cahr-TAHR-mee
  QUEL-lah cheen-TOO-rah pair
  fah-VO-reh Eh oon reh-GAH-lo

 Dov'è la cassa? *(Doh-VEH lah CAHS-sah):* Where is the cash register?

Today most of the stores accept *carte di credito* (credit cards) without problems (Visa and MasterCard, at least), but some of the small shops are keen on giving a *sconto* (discount) if you pay with cash (*pagare in contanti*). Some small or family-owned stores might also be willing to offer a discount if you buy a large amount of goods. There is no possibility of getting this discount in big department stores, but give it a try with friendly small-shop owners.

In Italy it is very important to always make sure to get your receipt, because you might be asked to show it outside the shop by some *ispettori della finanza* (sales tax auditors), and if you don't have it you may get a fine.

Unlike in North America, in Italy taxes are already included in the price on the tag, so no extra costs will be added at checkout. The price on the tag, or the price you are told by the shop owner, will be the final price.

Quanto costa?

QUAHN-toh CO-stah

How much is it?

**Posso pagare con la carta
di credito?**

POS-so pah-GAH-reh kohn lah
CAR-tah dee CREH-dee-toh

Can I pay with a credit card?

Ecco lo scontrino.

EC-co lo scon-TREE-no

Here is your receipt.

Potrei avere lo scontrino?

Po-TRAY ah-VEH-reh lo scon-TREE-no

Can I have the receipt?

Chapter 8

Grooming

 C'è un parrucchiere o un salone di bellezza in questo albergo? *(CHEH oon pahr-rook-kee-EH-reh oh oon sah-LO-neh dee bel-LETS-sah een QUEH-sto ahl-BAIR-go):* Is there a hairdresser or beauty salon in this hotel?

In Italian hotels you will find not only shops, restaurants, swimming pools, and saunas, but also fitness centers, dry cleaning/laundry services, beauty salons, spas, hair stylists, barbershops, and more. The use of the sauna and the swimming pool is normally free for all guests. The other services, though very convenient, are generally offered at a higher price.

L'hotel offre un servizio di lavanderia?

Lo-TEHL OF-freh oon sair-VEE-tsee-oh dee lah-vahn-deh-REE-ah

Does the hotel offer a laundry service?

L'albergo dispone di un fitness center? Lahl-BAIR-go dee-SPO-neh dee oon fitness center	Is there a fitness center in the hotel?
C'è una piscina/sauna in questo albergo? CHEH OO-nah pee-SHEE-nah SAH-oo-nah een QUEH-sto ahl-BAIR-go	Is there a swimming pool/sauna in this hotel?
C'è un centro benessere in questo hotel? CHEH oon CHEHN-tro beh-NES-seh-reh een QUEH-sto oh-TEHL	Is there a wellness center in this hotel?

 Potrebbe/Potresti suggerirmi un buon parrucchiere/ barbiere? *(Po-TREB-beh/Po-TRES-tee sood-jair-EER-mee oon boo-ON pahr-rook-kee-EH-reh/bahr-bee-EH-reh):* Could you please suggest a good hairdresser/barber?

If you go to Italy for a wedding or other special occasion, for a formal event, or for an extended visit, at some point you may need to buy toiletries or use the services of a hairdresser, beautician, etc.

You will find toiletries or hygiene products in beauty salons, supermarkets, and normally pharmacies. For the services of a hairdresser or beautician, a recommendation is often very useful. When asking a friend or relative for a recommendation, say: *Potresti suggerirmi un buon parrucchiere, per favore?* (Could you please suggest a good hairdresser?); use the polite form of the verb (*potrebbe*) if asking for a recommendation from someone unfamiliar. Remember that *par-*

rucchiere could be used for both female and male hairdressers, even though at times the feminine form *parrucchiera* is used.

Dove posso trovare un buon salone di bellezza?	Where can I find a good beauty salon?
DO-veh POS-so tro-VAH-reh oon boo-ON sah-LO-neh dee bel-LETS-sah	
Dove potrei comprare degli oggetti igienici e per la toilette?	Where could I buy some hygiene products and toiletries?
DO-veh po-TRAY cohm-PRAH-reh DEL-yee od-JET-tee ee-jee-EH-nee-chee eh pair la twa-LET-te	
Dov'è la farmacia più vicina?	Where is the nearest pharmacy?
Do-VEH lah fahr-mah-CHEE-ah PEW vee-CHEE-nah	

 Vorrei fissare un appuntamento, per favore. *(Vor-RAY fees-SAH-reh oon ahp-poon-tah-MEHN-toh pair fah-VO-reh):* I would like to book an appointment, please.

The world of the beauty salon or the hairdresser in Italy is not much different than in North America. To avoid waiting for hours, it is appropriate to make reservations well ahead of time. Prices vary depending on the service requested; for a cut (*taglio*), for example, prices will vary from 15 to 18 euros depending on the length of your hair; a style (*piega*) is about 20 euros; a perm (*permanente*) is about 50 euros; highlights (*colpi di sole*) are also about 50 euros. Just as you might expect, a *salone di bellezza* or a *centro benessere* offer many more services such as manicure and pedicure, waxing (*ceretta*, *depilazione*), massages (*massaggi*), baths, facials (*pulizia viso*), etc.

Posso venire subito?
Can you see me right away?
POS-so veh-NEE-reh SOO-bee-toh

Quanto tempo ci vuole per... ?
How long will it take for . . . ?
QUAHN-toh TEHM-po chee
   voo-OH-leh pair

 Taglio, colpi di sole e piega, per favore. *(TAHL-yo COL-pee dee SO-leh eh pee-EH-gah pair fah-VO-reh):* Cut, highlights, and style, please.

Like fashion, hair styles change from nation to nation and over time; what's in (*alla moda*) today might be outdated tomorrow. And what may be fashionable in North America might be completely different from what's fashionable in Italy or in Europe, in general. Therefore, when at the hairdresser, don't be afraid to ask for his or her personal and professional advice: *Che tipo di taglio è alla moda in Italia?* (What haircut is fashionable in Italy?) or *Vorrei cambiare il look. Cosa mi consiglia?* (I would like to change my look. What would you suggest?) or *Vorrei tingermi a capelli. Quale colore mi dona di più?* (I would like to dye my hair. What color suits me best?)

Vorrei tagliate le punte, per favore. I would like a trim, please.
Vor-RAY tahl-YAH-teh leh POON-teh
   pair fah-VO-reh

**Potrebbe stirarmi i capelli,
  per favore?**

Po-TREB-beh stee-RAHR-mee ee
  cah-PEL-lee pair fah-VO-reh

Could you please straighten my hair?

**Potrebbe farmi la manicure,
  per favore?**

Po-TREB-beh FAHR-mee lah mah-
  nee-COO-reh pair fah-VO-reh

Can you please do my nails?

**Potrebbe aggiustarmi le
  sopracciglia?**

Po-TREB-beh ahd-joos-TAHR-mee
  leh so-praht-CHEEL-yah

Could you do my eyebrows?

 Barba e capelli, per favore. *(BAHR-bah eh cah-PEL-lee pair fah-VO-reh):* I would like a haircut and shave, please.

In Italian barbershops you will find a very cordial, pleasant, and infor-mal atmosphere. Barbershops are often a place to socialize.

Italian men also frequent wellness centers, spas, and beauty salons, and invest in a variety of personal grooming products. In Ital-ian culture, it is very important to present oneself in a respectable, professional way (*curare la propria immagine*).

**Vorrei tagliarmi i capelli, ma
  non troppo corti, per favore.**

Vor-RAY tahl-YAHR-mee ee cah-
  PEL-lee mah nohn TROP-po
  COR-tee pair fah-VO-reh

I would like you to cut my hair, but
  not too short, please.

Vorrei dare una spuntatina ai capelli. Vor-RAY DAH-reh OO-nah spoon-tah-TEE-nah aye cah-PEL-lee	I would like a trim.
Quanto costa un taglio di capelli? QUAHN-toh CO-stah oon TAHL-yo dee cah-PEL-lee	How much is it for the haircut?
Potrebbe dare una spuntatina ai baffi? Po-TREB-beh DAH-reh OO-nah spoon-tah-TEE-nah aye BAF-fee	Could you trim my moustache?

 Dove posso trovare una lavanderia self-service? *(DO-veh POS-so tro-VAH-reh OO-nah lah-vahn-deh-REE-ah self-service)*: Where can I find a laundromat?

Fare bella figura (To give a positive impression) is very important for Italians. The *bella figura* is also reflected in the way Italians dress. Therefore, it is good to be perfectly dressed even when going out with a friend or just going on a *passeggiata* (stroll) through the town. Make sure that the crease of your pants is perfect, that your suit is clean, that your shoes are well polished, that not a single hair on your head is out of place.

If you need to have your suit, shirt, or dress cleaned, look for a *lavanderia* or *lavaggio a secco*. These establishments will not only clean and iron your clothes but will also make alterations. Of course, alterations can also be made by a tailor.

Potrebbe pulirmi questo vestito?   Could I have this suit cleaned?
Po-TREB-beh poo-LEER-mee
   QUEH-sto veh-STEE-toh

Potrebbe lavarmi e stirare   Could you wash and iron this shirt?
   questa camicia?
Po-TREB-beh lah-VAHR-mee eh
   stee-RAH-reh QUEH-stah
   cah-MEE-chah

Potrebbe accorciarmi questi   Could you please shorten these pants
   pantaloni e restringermi   and take in this skirt for me?
   questa gonna, per favore?
Po-TREB-beh ac-cor-CHAHR-mee
   QUEH-stee pahn-tah-LOH-nee eh
   reh-STREEN-jair-mee QUEH-stah
   GOHN-nah pair fah-VO-reh

Quando sarà pronto?   When will it be ready?
QUAHN-doh sah-RAH PRON-toh

Chapter 9

Shopping for Food

C'è un supermercato qui vicino? *(CHEH oon soo-pair-mair-CAH-toh kwee vee-CHEE-no):* Is there a supermarket around here?

Supermarkets (*supermercati*) have become very popular in Italy only in the past ten to fifteen years, as before Italians preferred to do their grocery shopping in the local *generi alimentari* (grocery store). Italian supermarkets are no different from those in North America in both the selection of products and the organization of their sections. Very popular supermarket chains are Copp, Sigma, and Sma.

More recently, many Italians have started to do their grocery shopping also at the *ipermercati*, superstores that sell just about everything, from food items (meat, cheese, deli, bread, frozen food, drinks, wines, beer, etc.) to games for children, home and garden furnishing items, appliances, perfumes, personal items, household cleaning items, over-the-counter medicines, shoes, clothing, etc.

You will find small supermarkets in urban areas. *Ipermercati* and large *supermercati* are usually located outside urban areas near highways (*autostrade*) or freeways (*superstrade*), and they offer ample parking.

In the *supermercati* and *ipermercati*, prices are cheaper than in local grocery stores or specialized food stores, though the quality is still excellent. Because of their location, supermarkets are mostly used for weekly grocery shopping, while the daily shopping is done at the *generi alimentari* or at specialized stores.

When shopping in these stores, check for specials (*sconti*) in the weekly flyer. If you become a regular shopper in a store, ask for a reward card.

Online grocery shopping is also a reality in Italy today.

Supermarkets are normally open from 9:00 A.M. to 8:30 P.M. Some *ipermercati* may stay open until 10:00 P.M., and may also be open on Sunday.

Dove si trova il più vicino ipermercato?	Where is the closest superstore?
DO-veh see TRO-vah eel PEW vee-CHEE-no ee-pair-mair-CAH-toh	
Dove sono i carrelli per la spesa/ cestini-spesa?	Where are the shopping carts/ shopping baskets?
DO-veh SO-no ee cahr-REL-lee pair lah SPEH-sah/cheh-STEE-nee-SPEH-sah	
Potrei avere per favore un flyer/ volantino pubblicitario?	Could I please have a flyer?
Po-TRAY ah-VEH-reh pair fah-VO-reh oon flyer/vo-lahn-TEE-no poob-blee-chee-TAH-ree-oh	

Dov'è il reparto gastronomia? *(Do-VEH eel reh-PAHR-toh gah-stro-no-MEE-ah):* Where is the deli section?

Here are some of the food sections found in a supermarket: *panetteria* (bakery), *ortofrutta* (fruit and vegetables), *macelleria* (meat), and *gastronomia* (literally, "gastronomy section"), which includes dairy products, deli products, and other homemade specialties. Supermarkets, as well as smaller grocery stores, carry a large selection of gluten-free items, too.

Note that since 2005 Italian supermarkets are allowed to sell *farmaci da banco* (over-the-counter medicines).

Dov'è la sezione frutta e verdura?   Where is the produce section?
Do-VEH lah seh-tsee-OH-neh
    FROOT-tah eh vehr-DUH-ra

Avete un reparto farmacia?   Do you have a pharmacy (section)?
Ah-VHE-te oon reh-PAHR-toh
    fahr-mah-CHEE-ah

Dov'è il bancone pescheria?   Where is the seafood section?
Do-VEH eel bahn-KOH-neh
    pehs-keh-REE-ah

Dov'è il Servizio Clienti?   Where is Customer Service?
Do-VEH eel sehr-VEE-tsee-oh
    clee-EHN-tee

Per favore, potrebbe indicarmi il negozio di generi alimentari più vicino? *(Pair fah-VO-reh po-TREB-beh een-dee-CAHR-mee eel neh-GOH-tsee-oh dee JEH-neh-ree ah-lee-mehn-TAH-ree PEW vee-CHEE-no):* Could you please tell me where the closest grocery store is?

Many Italians, particularly those living in small towns, prefer to do their daily grocery shopping at the local *generi alimentari* (grocery store), where the selection is limited, however. These stores normally carry dry goods such as pasta and canned food; dairy products; cold cuts; household cleaning items; hygiene products; drinks, wine, beer, liquor; etc. They normally do not carry meat or fish; some of them might not even carry fruits and vegetables. To buy specialized items Italians go to the *macelleria* (butcher shop), *fruttivendolo* or *frutta e verdura* (fruit and vegetable shop), *panetteria* (bakery), *pescheria* (fish market), *salumeria* (deli store), *pasticceria* (pastry shop), and *gelateria* (ice-cream parlor).

Grocery store hours vary; they are normally open Monday through Friday, from 8:00 A.M. to 1:00 P.M. and then from 5:00 P.M. to 8:00 P.M. By law, they must be closed on Sunday and on public holidays as well as one other day during the week, on a rotation basis with other grocery stores throughout the area.

In quale scaffale trovo la pasta?
Een QUAH-leh scaf-FAH-leh
   TRO-vo lah PAH-stah

In which aisle do I find pasta?

Vendete prodotti surgelati?
Vehn-DEH-teh pro-DOT-tee
   soor-jeh-LAH-tee

Do you sell any frozen food?

Potrei avere una cassa d'acqua minerale, per favore?
Po-TRAY ah-VEH-reh OO-nah CAS-sah DAK-koo-ah mee-neh-RAH-leh pair fah-VO-reh

Could I please have a case of mineral water?

Avete delle offerte speciali?
Ah-VEH-teh DEL-leh of-FAIR-teh speh-CHAH-lee

Do you offer any specials?

 Che giorno è il mercato all'aperto? *(Keh JOR-no eh eel mair-CAH-toh ahl-ah-PAIR-toh):* Which day is the open-air market?

Italians like to shop at the open-air market or farmers' market. In major cities there is a daily open market, while in many small Italian towns the markets take place once a week, normally in the town square. In the open-air market you will find all types of vendors, from food to shoes, from clothes to paintings, from household items to hygiene products.

A trip to the market is an experience you should not miss, even if you have no intention of buying. If you plan to buy something, browse first and check for quality but also for the best prices and *occasionissime* or *sconti* (bargains). Prices, even when indicated by a price tag or told to you by the vendor, are normally inflated; be sure to bargain down the price.

The quality of food is excellent at the open-air markets, especially dairy and deli products as they are often homemade. Fruits and vegetables, homemade sweets, preserves and marinated items are also of the highest quality. Meat and poultry are excellent buys.

Il prezzo è un po' troppo alto.	The price is a bit too high.
Eel PRETS-so eh oon po TROP-po AHL-toh	
Potrebbe farmi un prezzo migliore, per favore?	Could you please give me a better price?
Po-TREB-beh FAHR-mee oon PRETS-so meel-YOHR-eh pair fah-VO-reh	
Lo prendo, se abbassa ancora il prezzo.	I'll buy it, if you lower the price a bit more.
Lo PREHN-doh seh ab-BAS-sah ahn-CO-rah eel PRETS-so	
Se ne prendo due, mi fa uno sconto?	If I buy two, can you give a discount?
Seh neh PREHN-doh DOO-eh mee fah OO-no SCON-toh	

 Mezzo chilo di pane, per favore. (*METS-so KEE-lo dee PAH-neh pair fah-VO-reh*): A loaf (half kilo) of bread, please.

Bread is one of the food staples of Italy, but it is also one of the food items that has the most variation in ingredients, quantity, and shape. Bread making in Italy is an art. Often bread is identified as *pane regionale* (*pane toscano, pane calabrese, pane pugliese*) or as *pane locale* (*pane ferrarese*); other times the bread takes its name from its shape (*pane rotondo, filoncino, ciabatta*) or by the ingredients (*pane di semola, pane integrale, pane di mais, pane di segala, pane di orzo, pane di riso, pane di glutine*). Special and often decorative bread is also prepared for many holidays and festivity days such as St. Anthony, St. Joseph, All Souls', Easter, and Christmas, or for events such as births and weddings. Some common specialty breads include *pane alle olive*, *pane con uova*, *pane con alici*, etc. Many are called the regional names for bread: *la michetta*, *la biova*, *la pagnotta*, *la mafalda*. You may also have the *pane insipido* (unsalted bread, typical in Tuscany), the *pane arabo* or *pane pita*, and the *piadina* (a variation of the pita bread, typical in Emilia Romagna).

Besides grocery stores and supermarkets, breads can be bought in the local *panetteria*, *panificio*, or *forno*, which normally open very early in the morning and close by midday. When buying bread, ask for a *mezzo chilo di pane* or *un chilo di pane*, or if you prefer, ask for a *panino*.

Potrei avere quattro panini, per favore?	Could I please have four buns?
Po-TRAY ah-VEH-reh QUAT-tro pah-NEE-nee pair fah-VO-reh	
Ha del pane integrale?	Do you have any whole wheat bread?
Ah del PA-neh een-teh-GRAH-leh	
Un filoncino, per favore.	A French baguette, please.
Oon fee-lon-CHEE-no pair fah-VO-reh	
Quando posso trovare del pane caldo e croccante?	At what time will I be able to find hot and crunchy bread?
QUAHN-doh POS-so tro-VAH-reh del PAH-neh CAHL-doh eh croc-CAHN-teh	

95

Un panino con prosciutto e formaggio, per favore. *(Oon pah-NEE-no kohn pro-SHOOT-toh eh for-MAD-jo pair fah-VO-reh):* A bun with prosciutto and cheese, please.

In a *salumeria* you will find dairy and deli products of all types: prosciutto, mortadella, *salame*, *salciccia*, provolone, parmigiano, Romano, *crotonese*, *svizzero*, Gorgonzola, pecorino, mozzarella, ricotta, etc. Many store owners take pride in their homemade and genuine products with no preservatives. At times you may also find *piatti pronti*, a hot table, or you may be able to purchase delicious sandwiches with cold cuts. Sandwiches are also available at a *paninoteca* or *piadineria*.

Many *salumerie* will also offer a varied selection of grocery products such as pasta, *pasta di casa* (homemade pasta), *conserve* (preserves), *sottoaceti* (pickled vegetables), and *sottoli* (items in oil), *olive* (olives), *marmellata* (jam or jelly), *olio* (oil), *aceto* (vinegar), *caffè* (coffee), *vini* (wines), *liquori* (liqueurs), *acqua minerale* (mineral water), *insalata* (salad), *insalata di mare* (seafood salad), *supplì* (fried rice balls), *porchetta* (roasted piglet), *fritti* (deep-fried items), etc.

Duecento grammi di mortadella, per favore.
doo-eh CHEHN-oh GRAM-mee dee mor-tah-DEL-lah pair fah-VO-reh

Two hundred grams of mortadella, please.

Potrebbe tagliare il prosciutto a fette più sottili, per favore?
Po-TREB-beh tahl-YAH-reh eel pro-SHOOT-toh ah FET-teh PEW sot-TEE-lee pair fah-VO-reh

Could you please slice the prosciutto a bit thinner?

Potrebbe grattugiarmi un pezzo piccolo di parmigiano, per favore?	Could you please grate me a small piece of Parmesan cheese?
Po-TREB-beh grat-tood-JAHR-mee oon PETS-so PEEK-ko-lo dee pahr-mee-JAH-no pair fah-VO-reh	
La ricotta è fresca?	Is the ricotta cheese fresh?
Lah ree-COT-tah eh FREHS-cah	

 Mezzo chilo di spezzatino di manzo, per favore. *(METS-so KEE-lo dee spets-sah-TEE-no dee MAHN-tso pair fah-VO-reh):* Half a kilo of beef stew, please.

A *macelleria* specializes in meat and poultry products. However, similar to a *salumeria*, you will find many grocery items there. A *macelleria* takes pride in offering *carni scelte di prima qualità* (grade A choice cut), *insaccati e affettati di produzione propria* (homemade salami products and cold cuts). You will also be able to find a rotisserie service, which is actually more common in a *polleria* (poultry shop) or in a *rosticceria* (rotisserie and hot table). A *polleria* is a store similar to the *macelleria*, but is of course more specialized in poultry and dairy products. To be more competitive, many store owners combine in their enterprise *macelleria*, *salumeria*, *polleria*, and *rosticceria*. Many Italian *macellerie* offer among their products *carne equina* (horse meat); you will also find specialized *macelleria equina*.

Potrebbe darmi dieci cosce/petti di pollo, per favore?
Po-TREB-beh DAHR-mee dee-EH-chee CO-sheh/PET-tee dee POHL-lo pair fah-VO-reh

Could you please give me ten chicken legs/breasts?

Una dozzina di fettine di vitello, per favore.
OO-nah dots-SEE-nah dee fet-TEE-neh dee vee-TEL-lo pair fah-VO-reh

A dozen veal cutlets, please.

Ha delle costolette di agnello/maiale già marinate?
Ah DEL-leh co-sto-LET-teh dee ahn-YEL-lo/mye-AH-leh jah mah-ree-NAH-teh

Do you have any seasoned lamb/pork chops?

Quanto costa un pollo arrosto?
QUAHN-toh CO-stah oon POL-lo ar-ROS-toh

How much does a roasted chicken cost?

 Questo pesce è di giornata? *(QUEH-sto PEH-sheh eh dee jor-NAH-tah):* Is this fish fresh?

Italians buy fish in a specialized store called a *pescheria*. Because Italy is surrounded by the sea, the fish is normally *di giornata* (fresh, literally caught that day). For obvious reasons, many *pescherie* open early in the morning. In towns by the sea, freshly caught fish is sold in open markets near the seashore. Fresh fish is also sold by fishmongers who travel from town to town with their *furgoncini* or *autonegozi*.

Note that many fish or seafood restaurants are also called *pescheria*.

A quanto va il merluzzo?
Ah QUAHN-toh vah eel mair-LOOTS-so

How much is the cod?

Potrebbe darmi una dozzina di
   spiedini di gamberoni,
   per favore?
Po-TREB-beh DAHR-mee OO-nah
   dohts-SEE-nah dee spee-eh-
   DEE-nee dee gahm-beh-RO-nee
   pair fah-VO-reh

Could you please give me a dozen
   skewered shrimps?

Ha delle sardine in scatola?
Ah DEL-leh sahr-DEE-neh een
   SCAH-toh-lah

Do you have canned anchovies?

Vende pesce surgelato?
VEHN-deh PEH-sheh soor-jeh-LAH-toh

Do you sell frozen fish?

Un chilo di baccalà senza spine,
   per favore.
Oon KEE-lo dee bac-cah-LAH
   SEHN-tsa SPEE-neh pair fah-VO-reh

A kilo of deboned dried cod, please.

 Mezzo chilo di ciliege, per favore. *(METS-so KEE-lo dee chee-lee-EH-jeh pair fah-VO-reh)*: Half a kilo of cherries, please.

To buy *frutta di stagione* (seasonal fruit) or *verdura* (vegetables), visit the local *fruttivendolo* or *frutta e verdure* or go to the local market. In many small towns, you will see a *fruttivendolo ambulante* (traveling fruit seller), who will travel from town to town with his *furgoncino* (small truck) and a megaphone, inviting people to buy *frutta fresca e di stagione* (fresh and seasonal fruit). Becoming more common in the cities now are the *mercato degli agricoltori* (farmers' markets), where *frutta e verdura biologica* (organic fruits and vegetables) of the highest quality at very competitive prices are sold.

Un chilo di patate, per favore.	A kilo of potatoes, please.
Oon KEE-lo dee pah-TAH-teh pair fah-VO-reh	
Una cassetta di mandarini, per favore.	A case of tangerines, please.
OO-nah cas-SET-tah dee mahn-dah-REE-nee pair fah-VO-reh	
Vende prodotti biologici?	Do you sell organic products?
VEHN-deh pro-DOT-tee bee-oh-LO-jee-chee	
Un mazzo di rapini, per favore.	A bunch of rapini (turnip greens), please.
Oon MATS-so dee rah-PEE-nee pair fah-VO-reh	
Ha delle banane meno mature?	Do you have less-ripe bananas?
Ah DEL-leh bah-NAH-neh MEH-no ma-TOO-reh	

 Una dozzina di paste, per favore. *(OO-nah dohts-SEE-nah dee PAH-steh pair fah-VO-reh):* A dozen pastries, please.

Italians have an excellent reputation for baked goods. Each region offers a varied and extensive selection of *torte, crostate, dolci, paste,* etc. Each town takes pride in offering their local and original desserts, which may be purchased at the local *pasticceria.* Many *pasticcerie* take pride in announcing that theirs is a *pasticceria artigianale* (artisan pastry shop). The best time to visit a pastry shop is during special holidays such as Christmas and Easter, the St. Joseph feast, or the feast of the patron saint of the town. During these periods, pastry shops are at their best, even in their displays. The quality is always excellent, no matter what you buy: a *torta di compleanno* or *torta della nonna*, a *crostata di mele* or a *torta al cioccolato*, a *torta al gelato* or a *torta alla crema*, a dozen of *paste* or a dozen *cannoli alla ricotta*, some *sfogliatelle* or *zeppole*, half a kilo of *biscotti di mandorla* or *biscotti al pistacchio*, a *cassata siciliana* or some *cantucci toscani, torroncini alla mandorla* or *torroncini al cioccolato, cioccolatini* or *caramelle* or *confetti*.

Vorrei ordinare una torta alla frutta fresca.	I would like order a fresh-fruit flan.
Vor-RAY or-dee-NAH-reh OO-nah TOR-tah AL-lah FROOT-tah FRES-cah	
Potrebbe scrivere "Buon compleanno" sulla torta, per favore?	Could you please write "Happy Birthday" on the cake?
Po-TREB-beh SCREE-veh-reh Boo-ON com-pleh-AN-no SOOL-lah TOR-tah pair fah-VO-reh	
Potrebbe darmi mezzo chilo di dolci, per favore?	Could you please give me half a kilo of sweets/cookies?
Po-TREB-beh DAHR-mee METS-so KEE-lo dee DOL-chee pair fah-VO-reh	
Quanto costa questa scatola di cioccolatini?	How much does this box of chocolates cost?
QUAHN-toh CO-stah QUEH-stah SCA-toh-lah dee choc-co-lah-TEE-nee	

Un cono al cioccolato e nocciola. *(Oon CO-no ahl choc-co-LAH-toh e not-CHO-lah):* A cone with chocolate and hazelnut.

In Italy you will find prepackaged ice cream in supermarkets, local grocery stores, variety stores, etc. However, for a *gelato artigianale*, in a *cono* or a *coppetta*, go to the local bar, a *pasticceria*, or to a specialized *gelateria* to enjoy an ice cream of your favorite *gusto* (flavor) sitting down at a table. In the *gelateria* you will find a wide variety of *gelati alla crema* or *gelati alla frutta*, *gelati allo yogurt* or *sorbetti*, *gelati senza glutine* or *semifreddi* (partly frozen dessert), *gelati affogati* or *gelati drinks*, *tartufi* or *spumoni*, *granite* or *crepes*. If you are served at the table you will also enjoy the elaborate presentation of the ice cream with cookies, fruits, and similar toppings.

Che gusti avete?
Keh GOO-stee ah-VEH-teh

What flavors do you have?

Una granita al limone, per favore. A lemon granita, please.
OO-nah grah-NEE-tah ahl
    lee-MO-neh pair fah-VO-reh

Una coppetta ai frutti di bosco. An ice-cream cup with field berries.
OO-nah cop-PET-tah aye
    FROOT-tee dee BOS-co

Un semifreddo al caffè. A coffee *semifreddo*.
Oon seh-mee-FRED-doh ahl caf-FE

Chiuso per ferie. *(Kee-OO-zo pair FAIR-ee-eh):* Closed for the holidays/vacation.

Many Italians take their yearly vacations in July and August. Their preferred vacation period starts on *ferragosto* (August 15) and lasts two weeks. During this period, many Italian cities are literally deserted and stores are closed. Some stores might have special summer hours (*orario estivo*).

A sign saying *chiuso per turno settimanale* or *chiusura turno settimanale: mercoledì* indicates that the store is observing by law a day of rest taken in rotation with other stores. The sign *orario unico* indicates that the store is not closing for a lunch break, but has continuous hours. *Chiusura pomeridiana* means that the store will not open in the afternoon. Finally, *chiuso per lutto* means that the store is closed because of a death in the family.

Chiuso per le feste. Kee-OO-zo pair leh FEHS-teh	Closed for the holidays.
Orario unico. Oh-RAH-ree-oh OO-nee-co	Continuous hours.
Chiusura pomeridiana. Kee-OO-zoo-rah po-meh- ree-dee-AH-nah	Closed in the afternoon.
Chiuso per lutto. Kee-OO-zo pair LOOT-toh	Closed for death in the family.

Chapter 10

Eating Out

 Vorrei prenotare per quattro persone, per favore. *(Vor-RAY preh-no-TAH-reh pair QUAT-tro PAIR-so-neh pair fah-VO-reh)*: I would like to make a reservation for four people, please.

Italian cuisine is considered one of the best in the world; the so-called *dieta mediterranea* is also considered one of the healthiest diets. In Italy, *mangiare bene* and *dolce vita* go hand in hand; mealtime is also a way for a family to be together. Whether you eat at a very expensive restaurant or at a family-run *trattoria*, in a *rosticceria* (rotisserie), a *tavola calda* (hot buffet), a *pizzeria*, or at a *mensa* (cafeteria at a working place or university), you can enjoy authentic Italian cuisine. With the continuous flow of immigrants into Italy, restaurants offering international cuisine are more and more common. Still, Italians prefer their *dieta mediterranea*; they love home-cooked meals and generally dislike frozen food.

Until the 1990s, it was a rarity to find fast-food chains in Italy. However, things have changed now as Italians have created an Italian version of fast-food. A typical example are the many McDonald's restaurants in Italy (some of them are located in very historical places and buildings), whose varied menu is quite different from its North American counterpart and fits well with the Italian lifestyle of eating well. The most famous Italian fast-food chain is Spizzico.

A typical time for Italians to eat dinner at a restaurant is 8:00 P.M. or later; lunch is from 1:00 to 3:00 P.M.

Vorrei cambiare la mia prenotazione dalle sette alle otto.	I would like to change my reservation from 7:00 to 8:00.
Vor-RAY cahm-bee-AH-reh lah MEE-ah preh-no-tah-tsee-OH-neh DAL-leh SET-teh AL-leh OT-toh	
Purtroppo devo cancellare la mia prenotazione. Mi dispiace.	Unfortunately, I have to cancel my reservation. My apologies.
Poor-TROP-po DEH-vo cahn-chel-LAH-reh lah MEE-ah preh-no-tah-tsee-OH-neh Mee dee-spee-AH-cheh	

 Offrite un menu per celiaci? *(Of-FREE-teh oon meh-NOO pair cheh-lee-AH-chee)*: Do you offer a gluten-free menu?

To serve the always increasing numbers of people with celiac disease, many Italian restaurants offer gluten-free meals. If someone in your party is affected by this disease, it is always a good idea to specify your needs when calling the restaurant to make the reservation.

In case of allergies, use the expression *Sono allergico/a a...* (I am allergic to . . .). Use *-a* if you are female, *-o* if male.

Sono allergico/a ai frutti di mare.   I am allergic to seafood.
SO-no al-LAIR-jee-co/-cah aye
    FROOT-tee dee MAH-reh

Sono allergico/a ai latticini.   I am allergic to dairy products.
SO-no al-LAIR-jee-co/-cah aye
    lat-tee-CHEE-nee

Sono allergico/a alle noci.   I am allergic to peanuts.
SO-no al-LAIR-jee-co/-cah AL-leh
    NO-chee

Sono allergico/a alle uova.   I am allergic to eggs.
SO-no al-LAIR-jee-co/-cah AL-leh
    oo-OH-vah

 Potrebbe portarmi il menu, per favore? *(Po-TREB-beh por-TAHR-mee eel meh-NOO pair fah-VO-reh):* Could you please bring me the menu?

A complete dinner at a restaurant comprises: *l'antipasto* (appetizer), *il primo* (the first course; usually pasta or risotto), *il secondo* (the main course; meat or fish), *il dolce e la frutta* (sweets/dessert and fruit). At the beginning of a meal you may order *un aperitivo* (an aperitif); typical at the end of the meal is an espresso (often a *caffè corretto*: espresso with grappa, vermouth, or any other liqueur), a shot of *grappa*, an *amaro*, or a *digestivo* (digestif/after-dinner drink).

Many restaurants in tourist areas will offer, mainly at lunchtime, a *menu turistico*, or *menu a prezzo fisso*; these menus are offered at a convenient price and are excellent for tourists or office workers who want to have a very quick bite. The menu *a prezzo fisso* is also an excellent solution for dining out with a large group of friends or family. They normally consist of first and second courses with sides, and a small bottle of mineral water or a glass of wine.

You may also explore the *piatto del giorno* (special of the day) or a *menu vegetariano* (vegetarian menu). Children's menus are not very common in Italy.

Cosa è incluso nel menu turistico? What's included in the tourist menu?
CO-sah eh een-CLOO-zo nel
    meh-NOO too-REE-stee-co

Qual è il piatto del giorno? What is the special of the day?
Quahl EH eel pee-AT-toh del JOR-no

Offrite un menu vegetariano? Do you offer a vegetarian menu?
Of-FREE-teh oon meh-NOO
    veh-jeh-tahr-ee-AH-no

 Un bicchiere di vino rosso, per favore. *(Oon beek-kee-EH-reh dee VEE-no ROS-so pair fah-VO-reh):* A glass of red wine, please.

Italy is one of the top producers and consumers of wine, with each Italian region producing excellent wines. Italy's wines—such as Chianti, Barolo, Moscato, Valpolicella, Montepulciano, and Marsala, just to name a few—are considered among the best in the world. Wine classifications in decreasing order of quality are: DOCG (Denominazione di Origine Controllata e Garantita), DOC (Denominazione di Origine Controllata), IGT (Indicazione Geografica Tipica), and VDT (*vino da tavola*). With such an excellent variety of wine, it is more than appropriate to ask the waiter for advice by using the expression *Quale vino mi raccomanda?* (What wine do you recommend?). If you want to be more precise, ask, *Potrebbe raccomandarmi un vino rosso leggero?* (Could you recommend a light red wine?), or ... *vino bianco dolce?* (. . . sweet white wine?), or ... *un rosé frizzante?* (. . . a sparking rosé wine?) Note that the expression *vino della casa* (house wine) might not be recognized by Italians; as alternative, use *vino sfuso* or *vino locale.*

Besides wine, Italians drink a lot of mineral water. When ordering mineral water, specify if you prefer *acqua minerale liscia* (flat mineral water) or *acqua minerale gasata* (sparkling mineral water).

Remember when ordering that ice is not normally served with drinks.

Potrebbe portarmi la lista dei vini, per favore?
Po-TREB-beh por-TAHR-mee lah LEE-stah day VEE-nee pair fah-VO-reh

Could you please bring me the wine list?

Quali sono i vini della zona?
QUAHL-lee SOH-no ee VEE-nee DEL-lah TSO-nah?

Which are the local wines?

Potrebbe consigliarmi un vino per questo piatto?
Po-TREB-beh con-see-YAHR-mee oon VEE-no pair QUEH-sto pee-AT-toh

Could you recommend a wine to go with this dish?

Una bottiglia di acqua minerale frizzante, per favore.
OO-nah bot-TEEL-yah dee AK-koo-ah mee-neh-RAH-leh freets-SAHN-teh pair fah-VO-reh

A bottle of sparkling mineral water, please.

Una Coca-Cola con del ghiaccio, per favore.
OO-nah CO-cah CO-lah kohn del ghee-AT-cho pair fah-VO-reh

A Coca-Cola with ice, please.

Un antipasto misto, per favore. *(Oon ahn-tee-PAH-sto MEE-sto pair fah-VO-reh)*: A mixed antipasto [hors d'oeuvre], please.

In Italian restaurants you will find a variety of antipasti: from the antipasto *casalingo* (house antipasto) to antipasto *di pesce misto* (mixed seafood antipasto), from antipasto *di carne* (meat/cold cuts antipasto) to antipasto *vegetariano* (vegetarian antipasto), from the many types of *bruschetta* to the very popular *prosciutto e melone* (and melon). Even though the antipasto is supposed to be an appetizer, they are so rich and varied that at times they substitute for the main dish. It is common, especially in family restaurants, to order a platter with mixed antipasti to be shared with the other members of the group. To avoid unpleasant surprises, if you are not sure what exactly is in a specific antipasto, ask the waiter: *In che cosa consiste l'antipasto?* (What's in the antipasto?) Remember that with minor modifications you could use the same expression to find out what's exactly in any dish.

Potrebbe portarci un mix di antipasti, per favore?
Po-TREB-beh por-TAHR-chee oon meex dee ahn-tee-PAH-stee pair fah-VO-reh

Could you please bring us a platter of mixed antipasti?

In che cosa consiste l'antipasto casalingo?
Een keh CO-sah con-SEE-steh lahn-tee-PAH-sto cah-zah-LEEN-go

What's in the antipasto *casalingo*?

Come primo, gnocchi alla bolognese, per favore.

(CO-meh PREE-mo nyok-kee AL-lah bo-lon-YEH-zeh pair fah-VO-reh): For the main course, gnocchi Bolognese, please.

Because Italian food is very popular in North America and all over the world, words like spaghetti, fettuccine, linguine, lasagne, gnocchi, antipasto, pizza, bruschetta, prosciutto, espresso, cappuccino, latte, etc. are easily recognizable by non-Italian speakers, even if they are often misspelled or mispronounced. However, ordering a pasta dish in Italian restaurants can often be problematic because of the many types of pasta and the regional variation of names. To complicate things further, add the many different ways of preparing pasta dishes: penne *all'arrabbiata* (with spicy sauce), lasagne *alla bolognese* (with minced meat sauce), spaghetti *all'amatriciana* (spaghetti with bacon and cheese), tortellini *alla panna* (white cream sauce), spaghetti *alle vongole* (with clams), cannelloni *alla ricotta* (with ricotta cheese), etc. You can also order pasta with vegetables: pasta *e ceci* (and chickpeas), pasta *e piselli* (and peas), pasta *e fagioli* (and beans), pasta *e lenticchie* (and lentils), pasta *e fave* (and fava beans), etc.

Risotto in its many varieties is also very popular as a first course: risotto *alla Milanese* (risotto Milanese style), risotto *ai funghi porcini* (with porcini mashrooms), risotto *allo zafferano* (with saffron), etc.

For lighter fare, order as a starter a *minestra/zuppa* (soup), or a *brodo* (broth).

In Italy, pasta is always cooked al dente; therefore specify if you want your pasta to be *ben cotta* (well cooked). While in Italy, do not order fettuccine Alfredo (or pasta Alfredo) as they will not understand what you are ordering. Order instead fettuccine *alla panna*.

È pasta di casa?   Is it homemade pasta?

Eh PA-stah dee CAH-zah

Potrebbe mettere più formaggio, per favore?

Po-TREB-beh MET-teh-reh PEW for-MAD-jo pair fah-VO-reh

Could you please put in more cheese?

Si potrebbe avere un tocco di pepe e un po' di peperoncino?

See po-TREB-beh ah-VEH-reh oon TOC-co dee PEH-peh eh oon po dee peh-peh-ron-CHEE-no

Could I have a bit of black pepper and a touch of chili pepper?

In che cosa consistono gli spaghetti alla carrettiera?

Een keh CO-sah kohn-SEE-sto-no lyee spa-GET-tee AL-lah car-ret-tee-EH-rah

What's in the spaghetti *alla carrettiera*?

Come secondo, una bistecca ai ferri, per favore. *(CO-meh seh-KOHN-doh OO-nah bee-STEC-cah aye FER-ree pair fah-VO-reh):* For the main dish, a grilled steak, please.

It is common to ask the waiter how a specific dish is prepared and what kinds of sauces are used; in case of allergies it is imperative to ask, in order to avoid unpleasant surprises.

When ordering a steak, please remember that by default the steak will come *al sangue* (rare); to have it more well done, use the expression *ben cotta* (well cooked) or *al puntino* (medium).

If ordering fish, ask if it is *fresco* (fresh) or *surgelato* (frozen), and how it is cooked: *fritto* (fried), *a vapore* (steamed), *lesso* (boiled), *ai ferri* (grilled), *al forno* (baked), *in umido* (with a light sauce).

Main dishes are served with a *contorno* (side dish), such as potatoes and/or vegetables. Do not expect to be served a side dish of pasta or risotto as they are normally part of the first course. And do not necessarily expect a salad.

La bistecca ben cotta, per favore. A well-done steak, please.
Lah bee-STEC-cah ben COT-tah
    pair fah-VO-reh

Quali sono gli ingredienti in What are the ingredients in this dish?
    questo piatto?
QUAH-lee SO-no lyee een-greh-
    dee-EHN-tee een QUEH-sto
    pee-AT-toh

Potrei avere un'insalata mista, Could I have a mixed salad, please?
    per favore?
Po-TRAY ah-VEH-reh oon-een-sah-
    LAH-tah MEE-stah pair fah-VO-reh

In che cosa consiste il contorno? What sides come with my order?
Een keh CO-sah kohn-SEE-steh eel
    kohn-TOR-no

 E per dessert, cosa suggerisce? *(Eh pair des-SEHRT CO-sa sood-jair-EE-sheh):* What do you suggest for dessert?

Italian restaurants offer a great variety of seasonal fruits (*pere, pesche, mele, melone*), desserts (*tiramisu, cannoli, torta della nonna, mousse di cioccolato, torta di ricotta, crostata di mele,* etc.), ice creams (*cioccolato, vaniglia, torrone, nocciola, bacio, tartufo, cassata*), and sorbet (*sorbetto al limone, sorbetto di frutta mista*). Each region has its own specialty.

Italians usually end their meals with an espresso and/or a *digestivo* such as *grappa, amaro, limoncello,* or other types of liqueurs. It is also very common to order a *caffè corretto*, which is an espresso with a dash of liqueur. Never order a cappuccino after breakfast!

Instead of having dessert at a restaurant, it can be fun to go to the local *pasticceria* (pastry shop) or *gelateria* (ice-cream parlor) where you will probably find a wider selection of desserts and even better prices.

Potrei vedere la carta dei dolci, per favore?	Could I see the dessert menu, please?
Po-TRAY veh-DEH-reh lah CAHR-tah day DOL-chee pair fah-VO-reh	
Come digestivo gradirei un Amaro Averna.	As a digestif, I would like an Amaro Averna.
CO-meh dee-jehs-TEE-vo grah-dee-RAY oon Ah-MAH-ro Ah-VAIR-nah	
Un caffè corretto con cognac, per favore.	An espresso with a dash of cognac, please.
Oon caf-FEH cor-RET-toh kohn COHN-yac pair fah-VO-reh	
Una grappa, per favore.	A grappa, please.
OO-nah GRAP-pah pair fah-VO-reh	

 Il conto, per favore. *(Eel KOHN-toh pair fah-VO-reh):* The bill, please.

When you have finished your meal, ask for the bill: *Il conto, per favore / Mi porta il conto?* (The bill, please.), or informally you may ask *Quanto devo?* (How much do I owe you?) If you are in a hurry and would like to attract the waiter's attention, say: *Cameriere/a, Scusi...* or simply *Scusi*.

On the bill there will be a charge of a few euros for the *coperto* (cover charge) and *servizio* (service) to pay for service and bread. Therefore, Italians normally just pay the amount on the bill; they may round it up. Nevertheless, it would be appropriate to leave a 10 percent tip, especially if you enjoyed the service and the food.

Potrebbe portarmi il conto, per favore?	Could you please bring me the bill?
Po-TREB-beh por-TAR-mee eel KOHN-toh pair fah-VO-reh	
Quanto devo?	How much do I owe you?
QUAHN-toh DEH-vo	

 Scusi, ma io non ho ordinato questo piatto. *(SCOO-zee mah EE-oh nohn oh or-dee-NAH-toh QUEH-sto pee-AT-toh)*: Pardon, but I did not order this dish.

On occasion, even when eating in the best restaurants, the waiter might bring the wrong dish. To rectify the situation, use the previous Italian sentence or simply state back what was ordered: *Scusi, ma io ho ordinato...* (Pardon, but I ordered . . .).

Similarly, if you are unsatisfied with your order, inform the waiter by politely starting your sentence with *Scusi...*

Il cibo è freddo.	My food is cold.
Eel CHEE-boh eh FRED-doh	
La carne non è cotta abbastanza.	The meat is not cooked enough.
Lah CAHR-neh nohn eh COT-tah ab-bah-STAHN-tsa	

Questo piatto è troppo salato/ troppo piccante. QUEH-sto pee-AT-toh eh TROP-po SAHL-toh/TROP-po peek-KAN-teh	This dish is too salty/too spicy.
Mi pare che ci sia un errore nel conto. Mee PAH-reh keh chee SEE-ah oon air-RO-reh nel KOHN-toh	I believe that there is a mistake on the bill.

 Una pizza "Quattro Stagioni", per favore. *(OO-nah PEETS-sah QUAT-tro Sta-JO-nee pair fah-VO-reh):* A pizza "Quattro Stagioni," please.

Pizza could be considered the Italian version of fast food. Many Italian pizzerias (but also many other food places) offer their *prodotti d'asporto* (take-out products), the *servizio take-away* (take-out service) or *servizio a domicilio* (home-delivery service). In a pizza *al taglio* locale you can buy slices of pizza at a self-service table to eat there or to take out and eat while walking; in the *tavola calda*, you can buy a full pizza or part of it; in other similar locales, particularly in Naples, you will find pizza *a libretto* or pizza *a portafoglio*, where a small pizza is folded into four pieces and put in appropriate paper to be eaten while walking. Of course, you can always order a pizza to be delivered at home (pizza *a domicilio*) or order a pizza *da asporto* or pizza *take-away* (take-out pizza).

Besides the hundreds of varieties of *pizza bianca, calzoni,* or "regular" pizza (*pizza margherita, pizza marinara, pizza napoletana, pizza siciliana, pizza ai funghi porcini, pizza primavera, pizza ai cinque formaggi,* etc.), the majority of Italian pizzerias offer a full menu, from antipasto to dessert. Note that in the menu beside each pizza you will normally find the ingredients used.

Vorrei ordinare una pizza a domicilio, per favore.
Vor-RAY or-dee-NAH-reh OO-nah PEETS-sah ah doh-mee-CHEE-lee-oh pair fah-VO-reh

I would like to order a pizza for delivery, please.

Una pizza take-away, per favore.
OO-nah PEETS-sah take-away pair fah-VO-reh

A take-out pizza, please.

Un calzone ai funghi e prosciutto, per favore.
Oon cahl-TSO-neh aye FOON-ghee eh pro-SHOOT-toh pair fah-VO-reh

A calzone with mushrooms and prosciutto, please.

Quanto tempo ci vuole per il servizio a domicilio?
QUAHN-toh TEHM-po chee voo-OH-leh pair eel sair-VEE-tsee-oh ah doh-mee-CHEE-lee-oh

How long will delivery take?

Un caffè e una brioche, per favore. *(Oon caf-FEH eh OO-nah bree-OSH pair fah-VO-reh):* A coffee and a brioche, please.

Often Italians have a quick breakfast at the local bar. They normally order *un caffè* with *un cornetto alla crema* (a croissant with custard) or *al cioccolato* (with chocolate) or *una pasta* (a pastry). A *caffè* is actually an espresso, which is by default *ristretto* or *corto* (strong). For a more diluted coffee, order *un caffè lungo* or *alto*. Some prefer to order a *caffellatte* or a *caffè macchiato* or a *latte macchiato*. If you need something more solid, you may want to order a premade *panino* or *tramezzino*.

Note the appropriate and typical sequence to be served in a bar: First you pay *alla cassa* (at the cash register), where you will get *uno scontrino* (a bill), which you will redeem at the actual bar. The barista will serve you and will tear your receipt. Please remember that when buying something in Italy it is important to always request a receipt, because you might be asked by a *guardia di finanza* to produce one outside of the shop or restaurant. If you are not able to do it, you (and the owner of the business) will be subject to a fine.

Please remember also that no Italian will order a cappuccino after breakfast.

Un cappuccino ed un cornetto, per favore.	A cappuccino and a croissant, please.
Oon cap-poot-CHEE-no ed oon cor-NET-toh pair fah-VO-reh	
Un latte macchiato e un croissant al cioccolato, per favore.	A latte *macchiato* (with a dash of milk) and a chocolate croissant, please.
Oon LAT-teh mak-kee-AH-toh eh oon CRWAH-sahnt ahl choc-co-LAH-toh pair fah-VO-reh	
Un caffè macchiato, per favore.	A coffee with a dash of milk, please.
Oon caf-FEH mak-kee-AH-toh pair fah-VO-reh	
Un tramezzino al formaggio, per favore.	A cheese sandwich, please.
Oon tra-mets-SEE-no ahl for-MAD-jo pair fah-VO-reh	

Un vermut, per favore. *(Oon VAIR-moot pair fah-VO-reh):* A vermouth, please.

When Italians see a friend or someone they have not seen for a long time, they like to offer them *un caffè* at the local bar. Not accepting such an offer is considered impolite, unless of course you have a good reason or excuse. Remember that when Italians say *Vieni, ti offro un caffè al bar*, the offer is not necessarily for a coffee but could be for a drink, an aperitif, a mineral water, and even an ice cream. As a courtesy, even if invited, it is acceptable to insist on paying the bill, even though it is difficult to find someone who will actually allow you to pay. However, when possible, take the lead and invite the person for a drink yourself.

Se non ti dispiace, preferirei un'acqua minerale.
Seh nohn tee dee-spee-AH-cheh preh-feh-ree-RAY oon-ak-koo-ah mee-neh-RAH-leh

If you do not mind, I would prefer a mineral water.

Un aperitivo, per favore.
Oon ah-pair-ee-TEE-vo pair fah-VO-reh

An aperitif, please.

Un amaro, per favore.
Oon ah-MAH-ro pair fah-VO-reh

A bitter, please.

Un caffè corretto, per favore.
Oon caf-FEH cor-RET-toh pair fah-VO-reh

A coffee with a dash of liqueur, please.

Chapter 11

Entertainment

 Quale film proiettano questa settimana all'Odeon?
(QUAH-leh feelm proy-ET-tah-no QUEH-stah set-tee-MAH-nah al-LO-deh-on): What movie are they showing at the Odeon this week?

The Italian film industry has always been considered one of the best in the world. Fellini, De Sica, Bertolucci, Tornatore, Salvatores, and Benigni are Oscar-winning directors. Italian movies such as *Ladri di biciclette*, *8½*, *La dolce vita*, *Umberto D*, and many more are regularly listed among the best movies ever made. Many Italian actors, including Academy Award winners Sophia Loren and Roberto Benigni and three-time nominee Marcello Mastroianni, are known worldwide. Italian artists have also won Oscars in original dramatic score, costumes, and other categories. The industry is constantly producing excellent directors, actors, and artists in the international scene.

Italian movies do quite well at the box office, even though the market is dominated by American movies dubbed into Italian. You will not find many Italian theaters that show movies in English.

The cost for a movie ticket varies, depending on the day of the showing, from 4 to 5 euros for weekdays to 7 to 8 euros for Saturday and Sunday. If you need to make a reservation (online or by phone) for very popular movies, the cost is normally 0,50 euro more. Special prices or combo prices (tickets plus snack) might be available in some theaters. The price for a drink and a medium popcorn box is about 7 euros.

Potrebbe suggerirmi una buona sala cinematografica, per favore?	Could you please suggest a good movie theater?
Po-TREB-beh sood-jeh-REER-mee OO-nah boo-OH-nah SAH-lah chee-neh-mah-toh-GRAH-fee-cah pair fah-VO-reh	
Potrebbe suggerirmi un buon film comico/romantico, per favore?	Could you please suggest a good comedy/romantic movie?
Po-TREB-beh sood-jeh-REER-mee oon boo-ON feelm CO-mee-co/ ro-MAHN-tee-co pair fah-VO-reh	
Quanto costa il biglietto?	How much does a ticket cost?
QUAHN-toh CO-stah eel beel-YET-toh	
A che ora inizia/finisce il film/ lo spettacolo?	At what time does the movie/show start/finish?
Ah keh OH-rah ee-NEE-tsee-ah/ fee-NEE-sheh eel feelm/lo spet-TAH-co-lo	

Cosa rappresentano al teatro greco di Siracusa? *(CO-sah rap-preh-ZEHN-tah-no al teh-AH-tro GREH-co dee See-rah-COO-zah)*: What is playing at the Syracuse Greek Theater?

Italy has always produced excellent theatrical authors. Nobel Prize winners such as Luigi Pirandello and Dario Fo, together with Eduardo De Filippo and Carlo Goldoni, are among the best known dramatists in the world. Commedia dell'arte with its masks has influenced world theater for centuries. Many Italian cities have a *teatro stabile*; Italian theaters such Teatro alla Scala (Milano), Teatro La Fenice (Venezia), Teatro San Carlo (Napoli), Teatro Massimo (Palermo), Teatro Olimpico (Vicenza), just to name a few, are internationally renowned. Greek theaters such as the ones in Taormina or Syracuse, or the Arena in Verona, are still used for theatrical events. While in Italy you can enjoy all sorts of theatrical pieces, from Greek tragedies to Latin comedies, from commedia dell'arte to Goldoni, from Molière to Shakespeare, from Ibsen to Shaw.

Prices vary, from 15 to 35 euros, according to the theater, the company, city, play, and type of seat. For a premiere show or premiere theaters, prices are much higher. Special prices for students, seniors, schools, and groups are very common. Season tickets are also quite common.

During the summer, many towns offer free concerts, theatrical plays, and similar events of good to excellent quality.

Quanto dura lo spettacolo?	How long does the show last?
QUAHN-toh DOO-rah lo	
spet-TAH-co-lo	

Offrite dei prezzi ridotti per studenti/anziani?
Of-FREE-teh day PRETS-see ree-DOHT-tee PAIR stoo-DEHN-tee/ahn-tsee-AH-nee

Do you offer special prices for students/seniors?

Vorrei prenotare due posti in galleria/platea/un palco.
Vor-RAY preh-no-TAH-reh DOO-eh PO-stee gal-leh-REE-ah/plah-TEH-ah/oon PAHL-co

I would like to reserve two gallery/stalls/balcony seats.

A che ora è aperto il botteghino?
Ah keh OH-rah eh ah-PAIR-toh eel bot-teh-GEE-no

At what time does the box office open?

 Chi sono i protagonisti del musical? (*Kee SO-no ee pro-tah-go-NEE-stee del MOO-zee-cahl*): Who are the protagonists of the musical?

Even though it has its antecedent in the *commedia musicale* of the 1950s–70s, the musical, as we know it today, has a very recent history in Italy. The first long-running show was *Grease*, staged in 1997 in Rome and Milan; the show was a box-office hit. Since then, musicals have become popular in Italy, especially among the younger generation. Musicals are also an integral part of the entertainment in many tourist villages and resorts, which has contributed to the success of the genre in Italy.

Cabaret shows and shows by Italian leading stand-up comics are also very popular.

An average price for these types of shows is about 40 euros. For prices, show information, and the calendar of events, consult the

Spettacoli section in local newspapers, or search the Internet. Many theaters provide ticket sales online (*biglietteria online*) with an extra charge of about 2 euros.

È permesso l'uso della macchina fotografica/telecamera durante lo spettacolo?	Is the use of a camera/camcorder allowed during the show?
Eh pair-MES-so LOO-zo DEL-lah MAHK-kee-nah fo-toh-GRAH-fee-cah/teh-leh-CAH-meh-rah doo-RAHN-teh lo spet-TAH-co-lo	
Ha un calendario degli eventi per il vostro teatro?	Do you have a calendar of events in your theater?
Ah oon cah-lehn-DAH-ree-oh DEHL-yee eh-VEHN-tee pair eel VO-stro teh-AH-tro	

 Dove posso trovare informazioni sulla stagione lirica al Teatro alla Scala? *(DO-veh POS-so tro-VAH-reh een-for-mah-tsee-OH-nee SOOL-lah stah-JO-neh LEE-ree-cah ahl Teh-AH-tro AL-lah SCAH-lah):* Where would I be able to find some information about the opera season at the Teatro alla Scala?

Italian is the language of music and opera; Italy has exported this prestigious form of art all over the world. Italian words like *aria*, *concerto*, *allegro*, *adagio*, *andante*, *piano*, *soprano*, etc. are words recognized by music lovers around the world. Composers, artists, and singers like Verdi, Puccini, Donizetti, Rossini, Scarlatti, Monteverdi, Stradivari, Mascagni, Paganini, Palestrina, Vivaldi, Caruso, Pavarotti, and most recently Bocelli are all household names among music lovers. Operas such as *La traviata, Tosca, Pagliacci, Le nozze di Figaro, Madame Butterfly,* and *Turandot,* and arias such as "Nessun dorma," "La donna è mobile," "Che gelida manina," "Largo al factotum," etc., are all recognizable worldwide.

Prices for opera are quite expensive but not prohibitive, but you need to reserve your seat very much in advance. For example, in the renowned Teatro alla Scala in Milan, you might find tickets as low as 18 euros and as high as 126 euros. Of course, for premiere performances, the prices are much higher.

Quando è la prima della Turandot di Puccini?	When is the premiere of Puccini's *Turandot?*
QUAHN-doh eh lah PREE-mah DEL-lah Too-rahn-DOH dee Poot-CHEE-nee	
Quanto costa un abbonamento?	What is the price for a season ticket?
QUAHN-toh CO-stah oon ab-bo-nah-MEHN-toh	
Ci sono dei buoni posti disponibili?	Are there any good seats available?
Cheeh SO-no day boo-OH-nee PO-stee dee-spoh-NEE-bee-lee	

 C'è un festa in paese questo weekend? *(CHEH oon FEH-stah een pah-EH-zeh QUEH-sto weekend):* Is there a festival in town this weekend?

In the typical Italian town, during the summer, there is a different festival almost every weekend. Many are dedicated to the town's patron saint or other religious figures, but Italy also hosts many popular music and cultural festivals.

Mi piacerebbe andare a vedere il Carnevale di Venezia o il Carnevale di Viareggio.	I would like to see the Venice Carnival or the Viareggio Carnival.

Me pee-ah-cheh-REHB-beh
ahn-DAH-reh ah veh-DEH-reh eel
cahr-neh-VAH-leh dee veh-NEHT-
zee-ah oh eel cahr-neh-VAH-leh
dee vee-ah-REHJ-jee-oh

A che ora è la processione?   What time is the procession?
Ah keh OH-rah EH la proh-chehs-
see-OH-neh

A che ora sono i fuochi d'artificio?   What time are the fireworks?
Ah keh OH-rah SOH-noh ee
foo-OH-kee dahr-tee-FEE-chee-oh

Andiamo al concerto di Laura Pausini? *(Ahn-dee-AH-mo ahl kohn-CHAIR-toh dee LA-oo-rah Pa-oo-ZEE-nee):* Do you want to go to Laura Pausini's concert?

Young Italians, also in view of the high prices of theatrical plays, prefer to go to concerts, to go to the disco, to watch a soccer game at the *stadio*, or to spend free time with friends at a local bar. The price for a concert normally does not exceed 60 euros; a visit to a disco is about 20 to 25 euros and includes the admission and a drink; for about 50 euros you can get a good seat for a top soccer match.

Chi gioca oggi?
Kee JO-cah OD-jee

Which (soccer) team is playing today?

Dove si comprano i biglietti per il concerto/la partita di domenica?
DOH-veh see TROH-vah-no ee beel-yee-EHT-tee pair eel con-CHEHR-toh/lah pahr-TEE-tah dee doh-MEH-nee-cah

Where can one buy tickets for Sunday's concert/game?

 Dove posso trovare una buona discoteca? *(DOH-veh POS-so tro-VAH-reh OO-nah boo-OH-nah dee-sco-TEH-cah)*: Where can I find a good disco(theque)?

The minimum age to be admitted into a disco in Italy is eighteen; the minimum drinking age in Italy is also eighteen, but unfortunately the laws and controls in Italian discos are very relaxed.

Quanto costa un biglietto per la discoteca?
QUAHN-toh CO-stah oon beel-YET-toh pair lah dee-sco-TEH-cah

How much is a ticket for the discotheque?

Potrebbe suggerirmi un buon night-club, per favore?
Po-TREB-beh sood-jeh-REER-mee oon boo-ON night-club pair fah-VO-reh

Could you please suggest a good nightclub?

Un cocktail, per favore. *(Oon cocktail pair fah-VOH-reh):* A cocktail, please.

The most common drink sold in Italian nightclubs and discos are cocktails and aperitifs, not wine. These locales can serve alcoholic drinks until 2:00 A.M. Italy's production of beer is quite limited; the most popular beers in Italy are Peroni, Moretti, and Messina. Imported beers are also readily available.

Un aperitivo, per favore.	An aperitif, please.
Oon ah-peh-REE-tee-voh pair fah-VOH-reh	
Una Peroni, per favore.	A Peroni beer, please.
OO-nah Peh-ROH-nee pair fah-VOH-reh	
Una birra alla spina per favore.	A draft beer, please.
OO-nah BEER-ah AHL-lah SPEE-nah pair fah-VOH-reh	

 Cosa c'è oggi in televisione? *(CO-sah CHEH OD-jee een teh-leh-vee-see-OH-neh):* What's on TV today?

If you prefer to spend time at home, it may be fun to rent an Italian movie or enjoy a television show.

Movie rentals (*videonoleggio*) are less expensive in Italy than in North America; note, however, that you will be charged by the hour. Remember also that movie rental is not a very popular practice in Italy.

Besides sports programs, reality shows and variety shows are very popular in Italy. The most popular shows are aired on weekends.

Avete una guida ai programmi TV? Do you have a TV guide?
Ah-VEH-teh OO-nah goo-EE-dah
    aye pro-GRAM-mee tee-voo

Vorrei noleggiare un DVD. I would like to rent a DVD.
Vor-RAY no-led-JA-reh oon
    dee-voo-dee

Su quale canale si vede CNN? What channel is CNN on?
Soo QUAH-leh cah-NAH-leh see
    VEH-deh chee-EN-neh-EN-neh

Chapter 12

Tourism and Sightseeing

Potrei avere una cartina della città? *(Po-TRAY ah-VEH-reh OO-nah cahr-TEE-nah DEL-lah cheet-TAH):* May I have a city map?

The most important source of information for tourists in Italy is the *ufficio informazioni turistiche* (tourist information office). The office is normally located in the very center of each city, usually in the *piazza principale* (main square) or close to the *principale attrazione turistica* (major tourist attraction) of the area. Bigger cities and places with a strong tourist vocation might have more than one tourist information office, each located in a different area. In large cities, the *ufficio informazioni turistiche* is normally open every day, year-round, with longer *orari d'apertura* (hours of operation) during summer or festivities. In smaller towns, it may be that the office is open only for a few hours a day.

The tourist information office is a great source for tourists and people who are not acquainted with the city. There you can ask for *cartine gratuite* (free maps) and *dépliant della città* (city brochures), and you can buy a city pass to visit sites at a *prezzo scontato* (discounted price). In most cases you can book a *visita guidata della città* (guided city tour) and even ask for assistance in finding an *albergo* (hotel) or a *ristorante* (restaurant).

Vorrei qualche informazione sulla città.	I'd like some information about the city.
Vor-RAY QUAHL-keh een-for-mah-tsee-OH-neh SOOL-lah cheet-TAH	
Quali sono le attrazioni principali del posto?	What are the main attractions of the place?
QUAH-lee SO-no leh at-trah-tsee-OH-nee preen-chee-PAH-lee del PO-sto	
Saprebbe consigliarmi un buon ristorante?	Could you suggest a good restaurant?
Sa-PREB-beh cohn-seel-YAHR-mee oon boo-ON ree-sto-RAHN-teh	
Vorrei prenotare una visita guidata per due.	I'd like to book a guided tour for two.
Vor-RAY preh-no-TAH-reh OO-nah VEE-zee-tah goo-ee-DAH-tah pair DOO-eh	

 Due biglietti d'ingresso per il museo, per favore.
(DOO-eh beel-YET-tee deen-GRES-so pair eel moo-ZEH-oh pair fah-VO-reh): Two entrance tickets to the museum, please.

Italy is known all over world for its beautiful *musei* (museums) and incomparable *opere d'arte* (works of art). Almost every town, even the smallest, has at least one important place of interest or historic site. Main museums and the most significant tourist attractions are nor-

mally open year-round with one *giorno di chiusura* (closure day) during the week, in most cases on Monday. Most of these are also closed
on Christmas Day and a few other national festivity days. Some of the
lesser known sites and attractions may have limited *orari d'apertura*
(hours of operation), and it is a good idea to ask the tourist information office about that before heading to the site.

Museums have different *tariffe d'ingresso* (admission fares): They
usually have a standard fare for *adulti* (adults), then discounted fares
for *anziani* (seniors), *bambini* (children), *studenti* (students), *gruppi*
(groups), and in some cases for people holding a city pass. Sometimes
museums and tourist attractions have a *giornata a ingresso libero* (free
entrance day) for special occasions and events, so check with the tourist information office.

Most museums and tourist sites offer *visite guidate* (guided tours)
or *audioguide* (audio guides) at an additional cost. Sometimes *mostre
temporanee* (temporary exhibitions) are not included in the standard
admission price, so ask the *biglietteria* (ticket office) about it if you are
interested in visiting a special exhibition as well. In many museums
and tourist sites, you can find a bookstore selling books, gifts, and
souvenirs, as well as a bar or a restaurant.

C'è uno sconto per gli anziani?	Is there a discount for seniors?
Cheh OO-no SCON-toh pair lyee ahn-tsee-AH-nee	
La mostra di Caravaggio è inclusa nel biglietto?	Is the Caravaggio exhibition included in the admission?
Lah MO-strah dee Cah-rah-VAD-jo eh een-CLOO-zah nel beel-YET-toh	

Quando comincia/termina la prossima visita guidata?
QUAHN-doh co-MEEN-chah/ TEHR-mee-nah lah PROS-see-mah VEE-zee-tah goo-ee-DAH-tah

When does the next guided tour start/end?

A che ora apre/chiude il museo?
Ah keh OH-rah AH-preh/kee-OO-deh eel moo-ZEH-oh

What time does the museum open/ close?

 Scusi, come arrivo alla Cattedrale? *(SCOO-zee CO-meh ar-REE-vo AL-lah cat-teh-DRAH-leh):* Pardon me, how do I get to the cathedral?

Le chiese (churches) in Italy are a very important part of the *patrimonio storico e artistico* (historical and artistic heritage). Most of them hold precious *opere d'arte e di architettura* (works of art and architecture) and are worth visiting, no matter your religious beliefs. Most churches are open all day and can be visited freely. Those with valuable *affreschi* (frescoes), *dipinti* (paintings), or *sculture* (sculptures) may have limited hours, and in a few cases there may be a fee to visit certain areas of the church. Sometimes, the entrance is *vietata* (not allowed) during the *Messa* (Mass). In any case, please remember that these are religious places, and it is important to behave in an appropriate way: be properly dressed, *fare silenzio* (be silent), and respect the people who are there to pray. Also, make sure you are allowed to *fare fotografie* (take pictures) before you start snapping shots.

Quando apre la chiesa?
QUAHN-doh AH-preh lah kee-EH-zah

When does the church open?

Qual è l'orario delle Messe?
QUAHL eh lo-RAH-ree-oh DEL-leh
    MES-seh

What are the Mass times?

Si possono fare foto in chiesa?
See POS-so-no FAH-reh FO-toh
    een kee-EH-zah

Are photos allowed inside the church?

Dov'è l'affresco di Giotto?
Do-VEH laf-FRES-co dee JOT-toh

Where is Giotto's fresco?

✈ **A che ora parte la gita turistica?** *(Ah keh OH-rah PAHR-teh lah JEE-tah too-REE-stee-cah):* What time does the sightseeing tour leave?

Tourist sites offer various sightseeing tours. They can be *a piedi* (on foot) within the *centro storico* (historical center), *in pullman* (by bus) in large or more diffuse cities, or even *in battello* (by boat) in a few cases. Most tours are offered in several languages, but it is useful to know a few key phrases in Italian as well. Sometimes the tours will include some *tempo libero* (free time) to visit the site independently, but make sure to verify the meeting time and place with the rest of the group.

In Italy leaving *mance* (tips) is not a common practice, but it will be appreciated if you leave a tip for the *autista* (bus driver) or the *guida turistica* (tourist guide), especially if it was a long tour and they worked hard to ensure you enjoyed the city or site at its best.

Quanto dura la gita?
QUAHN-toh DOO-rah lah JEE-tah

How long is the tour?

Dov'è il luogo di ritrovo?
Doh-VEH eel loo-OH-go dee
    ree-TROH-vo

Where is the meeting point?

135

A che ora è l'appuntamento per il rientro all'albergo?

What time do we meet to return to the hotel?

Ah keh OH-rah eh lap-poon-tah-MEHN-toh pair eel ree-EHN-tro al-lahl-BAIR-go

Questa è una mancia per Lei. Grazie per il Suo ottimo lavoro.

This is a tip for you. Thank you for the great job.

QUEH-stah eh OO-nah MAHN-chah pair Lay GRAH-tsee-eh pair eel SOO-oh OT-tee-mo lah-VO-ro

 C'è una spiaggia libera qui vicino? *(Cheh OO-nah spee-AD-jah LEE-beh-rah kwee vee-CHEE-no):* Is there a free beach nearby?

Italy offers not only historical cities and cultural places but also great opportunities to enjoy oneself *al mare* (at the sea), *in montagna* (in the mountains), and *in campagna* (in the countryside). Italy has miles and miles of beautiful sandy beaches, which provide various types of entertainment to the tourists. If you are visiting a place by the sea and want to spend some time at the beach, either go to a *stabilimento balneare* or *bagno* (private beach) or to a *spiaggia libera* (free beach). To access a private beach, you must pay an *ingresso* (admission fee) to be allowed in.

Scusi, quanto costa l'ingresso?

Pardon me, how much is the admission price?

SCOO-zee QUAHN-toh CO-stah leen-GRES-so

Vorrei affittare un ombrellone e due sdraio. *(Vor-RAY af-feet-TAH-reh oon ohm-brel-LO-neh eh DOO-eh SDRAYE-oh)*: I'd like to rent an umbrella and two deck chairs.

To use umbrellas and deck chairs at the beach, you must rent them. Private beaches normally offer many services, like *bagni* (toilets), *docce calde* (hot showers), *cabine* (small beach huts for changing clothes), *giochi per i bambini* (games for kids), *intrattenimenti* (entertainment) like *tornei di beach volley* (beach volleyball tournaments), *corsi di ballo* (dance courses), and other amusements. There you can also rent a *canoa* (canoe) or a *pedalò* (paddleboat). At a free beach, however, there are no services—in most cases not even toilets or *docce fredde* (cold showers)—so bring your own umbrellas and deck chairs. However, in every seaside area there is at least one *spiaggia libera attrezzata* (free beach with services), where all the basic services are available for a fair price.

Potrei avere la chiave della cabina?

May I have the key for the hut?

Po-TRAY ah-VEH-reh lah kee-AH-veh DEL-lah cah-BEE-nah

Che servizi ci sono in questa spiaggia?

What kinds of services are offered at this beach?

Keh sair-VEE-tsee chee SO-no een QUEH-stah spee-AD-jah

Vorrei uno skipass giornaliero. *(Vor-RAY OO-no skipass jor-nah-lee-EH-ro)*: I'd like a daily ski ticket.

In Italy there are beautiful mountains, which can be enjoyed in winter and summer alike. During winter there are activities like *sciare* (skiing), *pattinare sul ghiaccio* (ice-skating), or *fare snowboard* (snowboarding). Large ski resorts also offer activities for those who do not like to ski. To hit the big slopes, either bring your own *sci* (skis), *racchette* (ski poles), and *scarponi* (ski boots) or rent them. You can rent *pattini da ghiaccio* (ice skates) and *tavole da snowboard* (snowboards) as well. Before skiing, however, you must purchase a *skipass* (ski ticket), which can be *giornaliero* (daily), *mattiniero* (for the morning only), or *pomeridiano* (for the afternoon only). There are also *skipass settimanali* (weekly) or *mensili* (monthly).

Vorrei affittare/noleggiare un paio di sci e degli scarponi.	I'd like to rent a pair of skis and ski boots.
Vor-RAY af-feet-TAH-reh/no-lehj-jee-AH-reh oon PYE-oh dee shee eh DEH-yee scar-PO-nee	
Quali sono le piste più difficili?	Which are the most difficult slopes?
QUAH-lee SO-no leh PEE-steh PEW deef-FEE-chee-lee	
Dove sono le piste di sci?	Where are the ski slopes?
DO-veh SOH-noh leh PEE-steh dee shee	
Dov'è la pista di pattinaggio?	Where is the ice rink?
Do-VEH lah PEE-stah dee pat-tee-NAD-jo	

Conosce qualche buon sentiero per fare del trekking?
(Coh-NOH-sheh KWAL-keh boo-ON sehn-tee-EH-ro pair FAH-reh dehl trekking): Do you know of a good hiking path?

Mountains can be enjoyed during the summer, too. In summer one can walk along the *sentieri* (pathways), enjoying the breathtaking scenery and resting in the *rifugi* (mountain huts) that sometimes offer great food and drinks for a good price. For more sporty types, there are mountain bike rentals and even *arrampicata* (rock climbing). Your hotel owner or the tourist information office can provide the information you need to enjoy your stay to the fullest.

Quanto ci vuole per arrivare al rifugio?	How long does it take to get to the mountain cabin?
QUAHN-toh chee voo-OH-leh pair ar-ree-VAH-reh al ree-FOO-jo	
Dov'è la funivia?	Where is the cableway?
Do-VEH lah foo-nee-VEE-ah	

 Vorrei affittare un bungalow. *(Vor-RAY af-feet-TAH-reh oon BOON-gah-lo):* I'd like to rent a chalet.

Whether you are in the mountains, at the sea, or in the countryside, a great way to live in close contact with nature is *fare campeggio* (to go camping). There are *campeggi* (camping sites) almost everywhere in Italy, where you can either rent a *bungalow* (chalet) or a *roulotte* (trailer), but you must bring your own *tenda da campeggio* (tent) if you prefer to camp that way. In busy tourist areas, campgrounds are quite large and organized, offering various services and entertainment.

Please remember, however, that camping outside proper camping sites in most cases is forbidden, so check with the local tourist information office about the proper locations for camping.

Scusi, c'è un campeggio qui vicino?

SCOO-zee cheh oon cahm-PED-jo kwee vee-CHEE-no

Pardon me, is there a camping site nearby?

Scusi, avete una piazzola per una tenda?

SCOO-zee ah-VEH-teh OO-nah pee-ahts-SO-lah pair OO-nah TEHN-dah

Pardon me, do you have a space for a tent?

Devo pagare per parcheggiare all'interno del campeggio?

DEH-vo pah-GAH-reh pair pahr-ked-JAH-reh al-leen-TAIR-no del cahm-PED-jo

Do I have to pay to park my car inside the camping site?

È permesso il campeggio libero in questa zona?

Eh pair-MES-so eel cahm-PED-jo LEE-beh-ro een QUEH-stah ZO-nah

Is free camping allowed in this area?

Chapter 13

Common Warnings

 Vietato fumare. *(Vee-eh-TAH-toh foo-MAH-reh):* No smoking.

When traveling, it is useful to know the laws of the country you are in and what they prohibit. In Italy, smoking is forbidden in all public places; therefore you cannot smoke in museums, restaurants, bars, train stations, airports, cinemas, and public offices. In most cases, however, if you must have a *sigaretta* (cigarette), look for an *area* or *zona fumatori* (smoking area): You will surely find one in train stations and airports and some large restaurants have them, too. Long-distance trains have *scompartimenti fumatori* (smoking compartments); however, smoking is absolutely forbidden on regional trains.

Dov'è l'area fumatori?　　　Where is the smoking area?
Do-VEH LAH-reh-ah
　　foo-mah-TOH-ree

Vorrei un tavolo per fumatori, grazie.

Vor-RAY oon TAH-vo-lo pair foo-mah-TOH-ree GRAH-tsee-eh

I'd like to get a table in the smoking area, please.

 È vietato bivaccare qui. Dovete andare via, per favore, oppure vi faccio la multa. *(Eh vee-eh-TAH-toh bee-vac-CAH-reh kwee Doh-VEH-teh ahn-DAH-reh VEE-ah pair fah-VO-reh oh-POO-reh vee FAH-choh la MOOL-tah):* Loitering is forbidden here. Please go away, otherwise I have to give you a ticket.

In Italy today, the city mayors have been given the power of promoting certain specific laws within their territory: This means that, for example, in Venice *è vietato dar da mangiare ai piccioni* (it is forbidden to feed the pigeons); while in some seaside towns *è vietato camminare in bikini nel centro città* (it is forbidden to wear your bikini downtown), and on the beach *è vietato giocare a pallone* (it is forbidden to play soccer or volleyball) as you may accidentally hurt other *bagnanti* (bathers); and in Genova *è vietato bivaccare nel centro storico* (it is forbidden to loiter downtown). As a tourist keep in mind that it is forbidden to buy things from *venditori ambulanti* or *vu cumprà* (non-EU street sellers who sell fake bags and other merchandise on the beach or in tourist areas; they use this broken Italian expression [literally "would you like to buy?"] when approaching potential buyers), and if a police officer catches you while making such a purchase, there may be a large fine.

Vietato l'ingresso agli animali.

vee-eh-TAH-toh leen-GREHS-soh AHL-yee ah-nee-MAH-lee

No animals allowed.

Si prega di spegnere il cellulare.
See PREH-gah dee SPEHN-yeh-reh
    eel cheh-loo-LAH-reh

Please turn off your cell phone.

Vietato mangiare e bere.
vee-eh-TAH-toh mahn-jee-AH-reh
    eh BEH-reh

No food or drink allowed.

 Attenzione al gradino! *(At-ten-tsee-OH-neh ahl grah-DEE-no):* Watch your step!

The Italian word that translates as "Be careful!" or "Pay attention!" is *attenzione*. The word is ubiquitous: It is easily found on signs around all sorts of public places, or heard in various public announcements.

Attenzione! Lavori in corso.
At-ten-tsee-OH-neh Lah-VO-ree
    een COR-so

Watch for construction! Work in progress.

**Attenzione! Treno in arrivo/
partenza/transito.**
At-ten-tsee-OH-neh TREH-no een
    ar-REE-vo/pahr-TEN-tsah/
    TRAHN-zee-toh

Watch for arriving/departing/ passing train.

Proprietà privata. Attenti al cane.
Pro-pree-eh-TAH pree-VAH-tah
    At-TEHN-tee ahl CAH-neh

Private property. Beware of the dog.

Faccia attenzione ai ladri!
FAT-cha at-ten-tsee-OH-neh
    aye LAH-dree

Beware of pickpockets!

Pericolo: infiammabile. *(Peh-REE-coh-loh in-fee-ahm-mah-BEE-leh):* Danger: flammable.

In Italy, as in many parts of the world, easily recognizable international signs are used. A yellow triangular sign with an exclamation mark is the common sign for general danger (*pericolo: generico*); a skull with two crossbones indicates poison (*pericolo: veleno*); flames indicate that the item is flammable (*pericolo: infiammabile*); an explosion sign indicates the item could easily explode (*pericolo: esplosivo*); lightning means high voltage (*pericolo: alta tensione*); a stick figure falling means of course that there is a possibility of falling (*pericolo: caduta*). Here are some more danger warnings:

Pericolo: tossico.	Danger: toxic.
Peh-REE-coh-loh tohs-SEE-coh	
Pericolo: nocivo.	Danger: harmful.
Peh-REE-coh-loh no-CHEE-voh	
Pericolo: dannoso all'ambiente.	Danger: damaging to the
Peh-REE-coh-loh dahn-NO-so	environment.
pehr l'ahm-bee-EHN-teh	
Pericolo: alta tensione.	Danger: high voltage.
Peh-REE-coh-loh AHL-tah	
ten-zee-OH-neh	

 Scusi, è permesso portare la macchina fotografica?
(SCOO-zee eh pair-MES-soh por-TAH-reh lah MAK-kee-nah fo-toh-GRAH-fee-cah): Pardon me, can I take the camera inside?

As a tourist in Italy, you'll surely find yourself in museums and other places of culture. It is important in these places to dress and act appropriately. You must *fare silenzio* (be silent), *spegnere il cellulare* (turn off your mobile phone), and in most cases it is not allowed to *fare fotografie* (take pictures) or *usare il flash* (use the flash). It is likely that even *entrare con la borsa* (bringing your bag inside) and *portare cibo e bevande* (carrying food or beverages) inside is forbidden as well. Therefore, it is good to ask what is allowed at the *biglietteria* (ticket office) upon entrance or to take a look at the *cartelli* (signs) which are usually located at the entrance of each site. Like more or less everywhere, *è vietato calpestare l'erba* (it is forbidden to walk on the grass) in certain gardens and near significant monuments. Remember, too, that if you have a dog, it is mandatory to clean up after it.

È permesso l'ingresso ai cani?
Are dogs allowed in?
EH pair-MES-soh leen-GREHS-soh
   ahee KAH-nee

Mi dispiace, deve spegnere
I am sorry, but you need to turn
il cellulare.
   off your cell phone.
Mee dee-spee-AH-cheh, DEH-veh
   SPEHN-yeh-reh eel chehl-
   loo-LAH-reh

La prego di lasciare la borsa
I kindly ask you to leave your purse at
all'ingresso!
   the entrance!
Lah PREH-go dee la-shee-AH-re lah
   BOR-sa ahl-leen-GREHS-so

Non è permesso entrare in chiesa
You are not allowed in church
in pantaloncini corti/
   wearing shorts/a miniskirt.
minigonna.
Non EH pair-MES-so ehn-TRAH-reh
   een kee-EH-sa een pahn-tah-lon-
   CHEE-nee KOHR-tee/mee-nee-
   GOHN-nah

Chapter 14

Emergencies

 Dov'è l'ufficio della Polizia Municipale? *(Doh-VEH loof-FEET-cho DEL-la Po-lee-TSEE-ah Moo-nee-chee-PAH-leh):* Where is the office of the municipal police?

In the majority of Italian towns, the offices of the *polizia municipale* are located in City Hall, as this police force is responsible to the mayor. Their main duties are the application of norms and regulations of the towns; they are generally limited to public order, traffic, hygiene, respect for the environment, and the control of commercial establishments to ensure, for example, that they are open or closed according to their license and local laws. The *vigile urbano* is part of the *polizia municipale*. In the fifties and sixties, the figure of the *vigile urbano* became somewhat famous because of Hollywood movies; a *vigile* was always depicted as a folkloristic and eccentric traffic policeman, wearing an eye-catching uniform, hat, and white gloves, who, on top of a platform, directed traffic in Rome's busiest intersections. Today, however, you will see the *vigile* keeping an eye on the local neighborhood; controlling the traffic flow in busy areas such as schools, hospitals, and piazzas; giving tickets for traffic offenses; or patrolling the local open-air markets to make sure that the merchants have an appropriate license. It is also their duty to check the hygiene and source of the merchandise. Part of the mandate of the *vigili* is to intervene in case of a *scippo* (purse snatching), *borseggio* (pickpocketing), or *rapina* (robbery), and then collaborate with other *forze dell'ordine* (police forces) such as *Carabinieri*, *polizia*, and *Guardia di Finanza*.

Dov'è il Commissariato di Polizia più vicino?   Where is the closest police station?

Do-VEH eel com-mees-sah-ree-

    AH-toh dee Po-lee-TSEE-ah PEW

    vee-CHEE-no

 Dove si trova la più vicina caserma dei pompieri? *(DOH-veh see TROH-vah la PEW vee-CHEE-nah cah-ZAIR-mah day pohm-pee-EH-ree):* Where is the nearest fire station?

The various police forces previously mentioned are responsible to the Ministries of Defense (*Carabinieri*), of the Interior (*polizia*), and of Finances (*Guardia di Finanza*). The *Carabinieri* and the *polizia* have different duties, even though it is very difficult to identify those differences. For passport (*passaporto*) issues, firearms, residence permits (*permesso di soggiorno*), and immigration issues, the authority is the *polizia*. It is also the *polizia* (specifically the *polizia stradale*, road police) that handles traffic accidents and violations. Almost every town in Italy has a *Comando* or *caserma dei Carabinieri*; while you will find a *questura* or *commissariato/stazione di polizia* only in the major cities towns.

Quite different and clear are the specific duties of the *Guardia di Finanza* (finance police), who exercise their control along the borders, and are in charge of financial inquiries, tax evasion, money laundering, etc.

Other vital and essential security services are those provided by the *vigili del fuoco* or *pompieri* (firemen) and the *ambulanze* (ambulances).

È vicino la caserma dei Carabinieri? Is the *caserma dei Carabinieri* close by?
Eh vee-CHEE-no lah cah-ZAIR-mah
    day Cah-rah-bee-nee-EH-ree

 Qual è il numero del pronto soccorso? *(Quahl eh eel noo-MEH-ro del PRON-toh soc-COR-so):* What's the number for medical emergencies?

During emergencies, the faster help can be provided, the better. It is therefore important, should you find yourself in a situation where you must make an emergency call, to memorize or carry with you some essential emergency numbers. The most important emergency number in Italy is 113 (police and public emergency; this is the equivalent of 911 in North America). Other essential numbers are 115 for *vigili del fuoco* (firefighters); 118 for *pronto soccorso* (ambulance and health emergency); and 112 (*Carabinieri*).

The European Union has adopted the number 112 for S.O.S. In Italy, since March 2008, the number has been introduced gradually, into a few provinces at a time. Until the process is complete, the 112 number will operate alongside the existing national numbers previously described.

Anyone is able to call all emergency numbers for free from any phone. However, only call these numbers in case of real emergencies. When calling, the best way to convey the sense of urgency is to be direct and to ask that an ambulance, the police, or the firefighters be sent immediately. Otherwise, simply state that it is an emergency.

Si tratta di un'emergenza!/
   È un'emergenza!
See TRAT-tah dee oon-eh-mair-
   JEHNT-sah/Eh oon-eh-mair-
   JEHNT-sah

It's an emergency!

Serve un'ambulanza subito,
   per favore!
SAIR-veh oon-ahm-boo-LAHNT-sah
   SOO-bee-toh pair fah-VO-reh

We need an ambulance immediately,
   please!

Mandate i vigili del fuoco,
   per favore.
Mahn-DAH-teh ee VEE-jee-lee del
   foo-OH-co pair fah-VO-reh

Send the firefighters, please.

La polizia, per favore.
La po-lee-TSEE-ah pair fah-VO-reh

The police, please.

Telefoni al 113, per favore! *(Teh-LEH-fo-nee ahl chen-toh-treh-dee-chee pair fah-VO-reh):* Please call 113 (the emergency number equivalent to 911)!

If involved in an accident, stay calm, try to offer *pronto soccorso* (first aid) to those who need it, and call one of the emergency numbers for help. A quick response to the emergency could help save lives. Leaving the scene of an accident and omitting to offer first aid is considered a *reato* (criminal offense) and as such is punishable by law.

In case of an *incendio* (fire), call the firemen (*pompieri* or *vigili urbani*) and clearly state that there is an *incendio*. To warn everyone else in the building or to call for help from fellow citizens, yell: *Al fuoco! Al fuoco!* (Fire! Fire!) For a general emergency, shout *Aiuto! Aiuto!* (Help! Help!)

**C'è stato un incidente e vi sono
dei feriti!**

Cheh STAH-toh oon een-chee-
DEHN-teh eh vee SO-no day
feh-REE-tee

There has been an accident and
people have been injured!

C'è un incendio!

Cheh oon een-CHEHN-dee-oh

There is a fire!

Aiuto! Al fuoco! Aiuto! Al fuoco!

Aye-OO-toh Ahl foo-OH-co
Aye-OO-toh Ahl foo-OH-co

Help! Fire! Help! Fire!

 Qualcuno sta male! Presto, chiamate un'ambulanza!

(Quahl-COO-no stah MAH-leh PREH-sto kee-ah-MAH-teh oon-ahm-boo-LAHNT-sah): Someone is sick! Hurry, call an ambulance!

If someone is hurt, wounded, or suddenly feels very sick, the time before the arrival of a doctor or of an ambulance is critical and of the utmost importance for the patient. If you are a doctor or you know first aid (*primo soccorso*), your help might save a life.

So fare i primi soccorsi!

Soh FAH-reh ee PREE-mee
sohc-COHR-zee

I know first aid!

Sono un dottore.

SO-no oon doht-TOH-reh

I am a doctor.

**Sto male: vi prego di portarmi
in ospedale.**

Stoh MAH-leh vee PREH-go dee
pohr-TAR-mee in oh-speh-DAH-leh

I do not feel well: please take me to
the hospital.

Mi hanno rubato la macchina. *(Mee AHN-no roo-BAH-toh lah MAK-kee-nah):* My car was stolen.

While traveling by car, there is always the fear that your car could be stolen—even if it has the latest *sistema antifurto* (antitheft devices)— or damaged. In such a case, you will likely be covered by the car-rental insurance. The scenario could be worse if your purse, wallet, passport, or credit cards are stolen or lost. In all cases, report these incidents to the authorities within forty-eight hours; the number to call is either 112 or 113. You will probably have to file a *denuncia* (report).

While traveling, please remember that these types of stressful situations can be avoided by taking precautions and always being alert, especially in crowded places. Depending on the situation, even before calling the police, inform your credit card company or cell phone company, etc., of the stolen item(s).

Mi hanno danneggiato la macchina!	My car was damaged!
Mee AHN-no dan-ned-JAH-toh lah MAK-kee-nah	
Mi hanno scippato la borsa/ il portafoglio/il cellulare. Vorrei fare una denuncia!	My purse/wallet/cellular phone was stolen. I would like to file a report!
Mee AHN-no sheep-PAH-toh lah BOR-sah/eel por-tah-FOL-yo/eel chel-loo-LAH-reh Vor-RAY FAH-reh OO-nah deh-NOON-chah	

Ho perso il passaporto/la patente/ la carta di credito.
Oh PAIR-so eel pas-sah-POR-toh/lah
    pah-TEHN-teh/lah CAHR-tah dee
    CREH-dee-toh

I lost my passport/driver's license/ credit card.

C'è stata una rapina.
Cheh STAH-tah OO-nah rah-PEE-nah

There has been a robbery.

 Dov'è l'ufficio della guardia medica? *(DO-VEH loof-FEE-cho DEL-lah goo-AHR-dee-ah MEH-dee-cah)*: Where is the after-hours medical clinic?

All Italian towns have a *servizio di guardia medica* or *Continuità Assistenziale*. It is a free service that guarantees medical emergency service after hours. To use the service call the office for an appointment or directly go to the clinic; a house call is also a possibility. The *guardia medica* is open when all other medical offices are closed so that people have access to medical services twenty-four hours a day.

Potrebbe fare una visita a domicilio? Sono troppo malato.
Po-TREB-beh FAH-reh OO-nah VEE-zee-tah ah doh-mee-CHEE-lee-oh
    SO-no TROP-po mah-LAH-toh

Could you please make a house call? I am too ill.

Chapter 15

Health Issues

 C'è un ospedale qui vicino? *(Cheh oon os-peh-DAH-leh kwee vee-CHEE-no):* Is there a hospital close by?

The World Health Organization ranked the Italian health system as the second best in the world, after France. However, public opinion in Italy is in stark contrast with this report. The same organization places Italy in sixth place for life expectancy.

In Italy every citizen is guaranteed free medical assistance. A health card gives them access to the Servizio Sanitario Nazionale (SSN) and therefore to medicines (*farmaci, medicine*), visits to doctors and specialists (*visite specialistiche*), diagnostic exams, hospital admission, etc. Essential examinations and *farmaci indispensabili* (indispensable medicines) are free for all. All diagnostic tests, specialist visits, and *farmaci non indispensabili* (dispensable medicines) must be paid for, unless they fall into one of the exempted categories (children under 6, seniors over 65 with a low income, the unemployed, and people with recognized medical conditions). Unless exempted, for dispensable drugs Italians pay *un ticket* (a user fee) plus the cost of the medicine.

In many tourist towns there are clinics just for tourists. The cost of each visit at the *ambulatorio* (doctor's office) is 15 euros; a house call is 25 euros. It is wise, before leaving your country, to acquire medical insurance to cover you while traveling. If you require medical services in Italy, be sure to obtain an invoice afterward. You will need it for the insurance claim.

For medical emergencies call the *pronto soccorso* (first aid) at 118.

Sono un turista e non ho diritto al Servizio Sanitario Nazionale. Quanto potrà costarmi questa visita?	I am a tourist and I am not covered by the Servizio Sanitario Nazionale. How much could this visit cost me?
SO-no oon too-REE-stah eh nohn oh dee-REET-toh ahl Sair-VEE-tsee-oh Sahn-ee-TAH-ree-oh Nah-tsee-oh-NAH-leh QUAHN-toh po-TRAH co-STAHR-mee QUEH-stah VEE-zee-tah	
Dov'è il pronto soccorso?	Where is the emergency room?
Do-VEH eel PRON-toh soc-COR-so	
Dov'è il reparto di cardiologia?	Where is the cardiology wing?
DO-VEH eel reh-PAHR-toh dee cahr-dee-LO-jee-ah	
Come arrivo al reparto di terapia intensiva?	How do I get to the intensive-care unit?
CO-meh ahr-REE-vo ahl reh-PAHR-toh dee teh-RAH-pee-ah een-tehn-SEE-vah	

Vorrei fissare un appuntamento con il dottore. *(Vor-RAY fees-SAH-reh oon ap-poon-tah-MEHN-toh kohn eel dot-TOH-reh):* I would like to make an appointment with the doctor.

If you are not feeling well and need to visit a doctor, tell him/her what your symptoms (*sintomi*) are. If you are not sure what is making you sick, start with general sentences, stating that you are not feeling well, such as: *Mi sento male*; *non mi sento bene*; *mi sento poco bene*. Of course, if you are able to identify the problem, expressions starting with *Mi fa male…*, *Ho mal di…*, or simply *Ho…* will definitely help in expressing it: *Ho mal di gola* (I have a sore throat); *Ho mal di testa* (I have an headache); *Ho mal di denti* (I have a toothache); *Mi fa male la pancia* (I have stomach pains); *Ho la febbre* (I have a fever); *Ho il raffreddore* (I have a cold); *Ho l'influenza* (I have the flu).

Mi sento male. Ho bisogno di un medico.	I feel sick. I need a doctor.
Mee SEHN-toh MAH-leh Oh bee-ZON-yo dee oon MEH-dee-co	
Dov'è l'ambulatorio medico?	Where is the doctor's office?
Do-VEH lahm-boo-lah-TOH-ree-oh MEH-dee-co	
Dottore, mi può prescrivere qualcosa?	Doctor, can you prescribe me something?
Dot-TOH-reh mee poo-OH preh-SCREE-veh-reh quahl-CO-zah	
Adesso mi sento meglio.	I feel better now.
Ah-DES-so mee SEHN-toh MEHL-yo	

Dottore, potrebbe suggerirmi un buono specialista?
(Dot-TOH-reh po-TREB-beh soo-jeh-REER-mee oon boo-ON speh-chee-ah-LEE-stah): Doctor, could you please suggest a good specialist?

If you should see a specialist, be prepared to pay the necessary fee. However, it is not always easy to get an immediate appointment with a specialist. In most cases, a specialist will give you an appointment only if you are referred by a doctor. Here are the titles of some specialists: *dermatologo* (dermatologist), *oculista* (eye specialist), *otorino* (ear, nose, and throat specialist), *pediatra* (pediatrician), *oncologo* (oncologist). Note that the Italian and English words are often very similar.

Dov'è lo studio del dentista?	Where is the dentist's office?
Do-VEH lo STOO-dee-oh del dehn-TEE-stah	
Vorrei fissare un appuntamento con un cardiologo.	I would like to get an appointment with a cardiologist.
Vor-RAY fees-SAH-reh oon ah-poon-ta-MEHN-toh kohn oon car-dee-OH-lo-go	

 Ho vomitato tutto il giorno. *(Oh vo-mee-TAH-toh TOOT-toh eel JOR-no):* I've vomited all day.

Although it is easy to express one's medical problems with general words such as those mentioned previously, it is problematic to describe the exact symptoms to a doctor or to a specialist (*specialista*). This is because symptoms are often vague, subjective, and intangible; furthermore, their description normally requires a specialized language and precise details. A good description can be difficult even for native speakers.

Avrà un'intossicazione alimentare. It is probably food poisoning.
Ah-VRAH oon-in-tos-see-cah-tsee-
  OH-neh ah-lee-man-TAH-reh

Ho la diarrea da due giorni. I've had diarrhea for two days.
Oh lah dee-ar-REH-ah dah
  DOO-eh JOR-nee

 Sono diabetico. *(SO-no dee-ah-BEH-tee-co)*: I am diabetic.

If you have an existing condition, it is important to check that your medical insurance covers this condition before traveling to Italy. It is also wise to learn the basic Italian vocabulary associated with the condition. Wearing an appropriate medical alert bracelet (*braccialetto di assistenza sanitaria*) or carrying a note in your wallet specifying your condition is essential and could save your life. *Braccialetti* for diabetes (*il diabete*), for heart conditions (*i cardiopatici*), for people with Alzheimer's (*l'alzheimer*), or epilepsy (*l'epilessia*), etc., are found worldwide.

Sono allergico a... I am allergic to . . .
SO-no ahl-LEHR-jee-co ah

Soffro di... I suffer from . . .
SOHF-froh dee

Sono epilettico. I am epileptic.
SO-no eh-pee-LET-tee-co

Sono cardiopatico. I have a heart condition.
SO-no cahr-dee-oh-PAH-tee-co

Sono incinta. *(SO-no in-CHEEN-tah):* I am pregnant.

The first trimester of pregnancy (*gravidanza*) is always the most delicate for a woman, because she must adapt to the changes in her body, but also because of the risk of miscarriage. When traveling during the first few months of pregnancy, women must take extra precautions. And at the end of the pregnancy there may be some discomfort. Before undertaking a trip during pregnancy, a woman should talk with her gynecologist (*ginecologo*).

Ho una forte nausea. Oh OO-nah FOR-teh NAH-oo-zeh-ah	I'm really sick to my stomach.
Ho un forte bruciore allo stomaco. Oh oon FOR-teh bru-chee-OH-reh AL-lo STO-mah-co	I have a strong heartburn.

 Dov'è la farmacia? *(Doh-VEH lah far-mah-CHEE-ah):* Where is the pharmacy?

Pharmacies are not hard to spot in Italy as they are easily recognizable by a lit green cross. In small towns, pharmacies are normally located on the main roads or in the town square. If a pharmacy is closed, you will find a sign indicating which neighborhood pharmacy is on call (*di turno*). Please remember that pharmacies in Italy normally sell pharmaceutical products only and do not sell many of the items you normally find in North American drug stores.

Ecco la ricetta medica. EC-co la ree-CHEHT-tah MEH-dee-cah	Here is my medical prescription.

Mi servono delle aspirine, per favore.

Mee SAIR-vo-no DEL-leh ahs-pee-REE-neh pair fah-VO-reh

I would like some aspirin, please.

Ha pastiglie per la nausea?

Ah pah-STEEL-yeh pair lah NAH-oo-zeh-ah

Do you have any antinausea pills?

 Un piccolo consiglio, per favore. *(Oon PEEK-ko-lo kohn-SEEL-yo pair fah-VO-reh):* A little advice, please.

If you are not sure about a product in a pharmacy, ask the pharmacist (*il/la farmacista*). He/she will be happy to help you. If it is unclear how to use a product, ask him/her to explain how many times you must take the medicine and the dose. It is also important to disclose any allergies you might have.

Sono allergico al lattosio.

SO-no ahl-LEHR-jee-koh ahl laht-TOH-zee-oh

I am allergic to lactose.

Prenda questa medicina due volte al giorno.

PREHN-dah QUEH-stah meh-dee-CHEE-nah doo-eh VOHL-teh ahl JOR-noh

Take this medicine twice daily.

Le suggerisco questo sciroppo per la tosse.

Leh sood-jeh-REE-sko QUEH-stoh shee-ROP-po pair lah TOS-she

I recommend this cough syrup.

Ci sono effetti collaterali?
Chee SO-no ehf-FEHT-tee
cohl-lah-teh-RAH-lee

Are there any side effects?

 Dov'è l'erboristoria? *(Do-VEH lair-bo-ree-sto-REE-ah):*
Where is the health food store?

People have always turned to nature to find health remedies. In an *erboristeria* there are all sorts of natural products and health foods such as natural remedies, herbal teas (*tisane*), digestives and antiallergies, organic foods (*alimenti biologici*), natural hair products, etc. The old generation in Italy will always offer advice on how to cure your cold, your cough, your sore throat, etc., naturally. Homeopathy is the most common alternative medicine in Italy.

C'è una farmacia omeopatica qui vicino?
Cheh OO-nah far-ma-CHEE-ah
oh-meh-oh-pah-TEE-cah
kwee vee-CHEE-no

Is there a homeopathic pharmacy close by?

Ha dei prodotti antirughe?
Ah day pro-DOT-tee ahn-tee-ROO-geh

Do you have any antiwrinkle products?

Vorrei comprare delle vitamine.
Vor-RAY cohm-PRAH-reh dehl-le
vee-tah-MEE-neh

I would like to buy some vitamins.

Chapter 16

Making Friends

 Ci vediamo in piazza alle dieci. *(Chee veh-dee-AH-mo een pee-ATS-sah AL-leh dee-EH-chee):* Let's meet in the square at ten.

While in Italy, you will likely befriend some Italians. Since many Italians cannot speak English very well, it might be useful to know some phrases which you can use to interact with them or simply have fun trying to speak the language. Italians love to hear when foreigners try to speak their language. This can be a great way of making friends!

In Italy, especially in small towns, it is very common to meet people outside, either on the main street or in the most important *piazza* (square) in the city. In winter or summer, young people hang out there for hours and just spend time together doing nothing besides chatting. This may be quite different from what North Americans are used to, but it is definitely the most traditional way of meeting people in Italy, especially on a Saturday afternoon.

Nowadays young people are meeting in shopping malls, too, but the old trend of spending time hanging outside together still remains strong. Often, the main street or square is just the place to meet with friends to decide where to go afterward, but such a decision can take some time and you may end up staying in the square for hours! For older people it is more common to make plans in advance and meet directly in restaurants or other places, but in small villages the main—sometimes the only—bar can be a great way to meet locals, young and old alike.

Ti passo a prendere domani pomeriggio alle quattro. Tee PAS-soh a PREHN-deh-reh doh-MAH-nee po-meh-REED-jo AL-leh QUAT-tro	I will come and pick you up tomorrow afternoon at four.
Mi dispiace, ma domani sera sono occupato. Facciamo sabato? Mee dee-spee-AH-cheh mah doh-MAH-nee SEH-rah SO-no oc-coo-PAH-toh Fat-CHAH-mo SAH-bah-toh	I am sorry, but I am busy tomorrow night. What about Saturday?

 Che cosa facciamo stasera? *(Keh CO-zah fat-CHAH-mo stah-SEH-rah):* What are we doing tonight?

On Friday and Saturday nights, young people go to the disco or to nightclubs to meet friends or to make new ones. Discos normally dedicate Friday to young people ages seventeen years and up, while Saturday is for younger teenagers (13–16). The local bar, billiard, or video arcade is also an alternative location to meet and make friends.

Facciamo qualcosa tutti insieme domani?

Fat-CHAH-mo quahl-CO-zah TOOT-tee een-see-EH-meh doh-MAH-nee

Are we doing something together tomorrow?

 Mi dai il tuo numero? *(Mee DAH-ee eel TOO-oh NOO-meh-roh):* Can I have your number?

Italians are very friendly people and love chatting, so if you approach someone with a smile, you will be greeted similarly. Don't be surprised anywhere in Italy, though, if someone whom you don't know starts talking to you, making small conversation. Similarly, you may want to do the same. However, always remember to respect your interlocutor if he/she does not want to continue your conversation.

Breaking the ice (*rompere il ghiaccio*), while at a disco or at a night-club, is perhaps a bit more difficult, but the tactics are more or less the same worldwide.

Come va? Tutto a posto?

COH-meh vah TOOT-toh ah POH-sto

Ci conosciamo già, vero?

Chee coh-no-shee-AH-moh jee-AH veh-roh

Dove abiti?

DOH-veh ah-BEE-tee

What's up?

We've already met, correct?

Where do you live?

Mi fa molto piacere conoscerti! *(Mee fah MOHL-toh pee-ah-CHEH-reh co-no-SHEHR-tee)*: It's really nice to meet you!

If you are introduced to someone new it is important to *stringere le mani* (shake hands). Young people do not do it so often today, but if you do shake hands, you'll never go wrong. Really close friends and relatives *si baciano sulle guance* (kiss each other on the cheeks) upon meeting, especially if they haven't seen each other for a long time. And just like everywhere in the world, a *sorriso* (smile) is always appreciated.

If you are being introduced to someone new or if you are young and are being introduced to someone older than you, it is always appropriate to *dare del Lei* (use the *Lei* form of address) and to use *Signore* or *Signora* (Mr. or Mrs.) before their names. However, if you are young and are meeting someone of your age, you can easily *dare del tu* (use the *tu* form of address). After being introduced or after getting to know you, Italians will tell you *dammi pure del tu*, which means you do not have to use the formal *Lei* address with them any longer.

Ti presento il mio amico Marco.	This is my friend Marco.
Tee preh-SEHN-toh eel MEE-oh ah-MEE-co MAHR-co	
I miei amici vogliono conoscerti. Vieni che te li presento.	My friends want to meet you. Come and let me introduce you to them.
Ee mee-AY ah-MEE-chee VOL-yo-no co-no-SHEHR-tee Vee-EH-nee keh teh lee preh-SEHN-toh	

Il mio nome è John e sono americano. Mi piace molto l'Italia!

Eel MEE-oh NO-meh eh John eh SO-no ah-mair-ee-CAH-no Mee pee-AH-cheh MOHL-toh lee-TAH-lee-ah

My name is John and I am American. I really love Italy!

Come ti chiami? Non ho capito il tuo nome.

CO-meh tee kee-AH-mee Nohn oh cah-PEE-toh eel TOO-oh NO-meh

What's your name? I didn't get it.

 Esci con me stasera? *(EH-shee kohn meh stah-SEH-rah)*: Are you going out with me tonight?

Italian males are renowned all over the world as "Latin lovers" and in most cases they want to keep up with that stereotype. So women visiting Italy might be surprised at the forward manner of Italian men. Sometimes they can be very insistent, so women who do not appreciate this attention should be very strict and firm in response, which will be enough to make them stop. In any event, to avoid an unpleasant situation, remember that you are in a foreign country and be cautious. Men visiting Italy need only be kind to meet Italian women. If you are a man, these women will most likely expect you to *fare la prima mossa* (make the first move), which means introducing yourself to them and initiating conversation.

Usciamo a cena insieme?

Oo-SHAH-mo ah CHEH-nah een-see-EH-meh

Shall we go out to dinner?

Verresti al cinema/in discoteca/ a fare una passeggiata con me? Ver-REH-stee ahl CHEE-neh-mah/ een dee-skoh-TEH-kah/ah FAH-reh OO-nah pahs-sehj-jee-AH-tah kohn meh	Would you like to go to the movies/ disco/for a walk with me?
Sei molto simpatica. Mi piacerebbe conoscerti meglio. Say MOHL-toh seem-PAH-tee-cah Mee peeah-cheh-REB-beh co-no-SHEHR-tee MEHL-yo	You are a really nice girl. I'd like to get to know you better.
Vorrei rivederti, se ti va. Mi dai il tuo numero di telefono? Vor-RAY ree-veh-DAIR-tee seh tee vah Mee dye eel TOO-oh NOO-meh-ro dee teh-LEH-fo-no	I'd like to see you again, if you like. Would you give me your phone number?

 Mi sono pazzamente innamorato di te. *(Mee SO-no pats-sah-MEHN-teh een-nah-mor-AH-toh dee teh)*: I've fallen madly in love with you.

If you fall in love with someone in Italy, it might be useful to know a few words to surprise him or her. Keep in mind that in Italian the phrase "I love you" is usually translated as *Ti amo*, but this expression is used in a different way than the English. *Ti amo* refers to romantic love; therefore you want to use it only with your partner, only to address people you are passionately in love with. In English, "I love you" is used to address friends, children, or relatives, but you cannot use *Ti amo* for that: In such cases, use the phrase *Ti voglio bene*.

If you fall in love with someone, you will exchange *baci* (kisses), *abbracci* (hugs), and *carezze* (caresses); moreover you might call your partner *amore mio* (my love), *cucciolo/a* (little puppy), *piccolo/a* (little one), and other little words which you two can have fun making up. If you end up in a long-distance relationship, you may exchange old-fashioned letters, e-mails, or text messages: When writing to your loved one, use the phrases *mi manchi* (I miss you), *ho voglia di vederti* (I want to see you), *ho voglia di stare con te* (I want to spend time with you), *spero di rivederti presto* (I hope I'll see you again), *penso sempre a te* (I am always thinking about you), *mi fai felice* (you make me happy), and *sto male senza di te* (I feel bad without you).

Mi piaci molto. Sei una ragazza molto interessante.	I really like you. You are a very interesting girl.
Mee pee-AH-chee MOHL-toh Say OO-nah rah-GATS-sah MOHL-toh een-tair-es-SAHN-teh	
Mi manchi molto./Mi manchi da morire.	I miss you very much.
Mee MAHN-kee MOHL-toh/Mee MAHN-kee dah mo-REE-reh	
Sei molto bella. Ho voglia di baciarti.	You are gorgeous. I want to kiss you.
Say MOHL-toh BEL-lah Oh VOL-yah dee bah-CHAHR-tee	
Sei il ragazzo più bello del mondo. Fatti abbracciare.	You are the most handsome man in the world. Let me hug you.
Say eel rah-GATS-so PEW BEL-lo del MOHN-doh FAT-tee ab-brat-CHAH-reh	

Chapter 17

Keeping in Touch

 Un francobollo per gli Stati Uniti, per favore. *(Oon frahn-co-BOHL-lo pair lyee STAH-tee oo-NEE-tee pair fah-VOR-eh)*: A stamp for the United States, please.

Today there are many different ways to keep in touch with friends and family back home, but sending an old-fashioned *cartolina* (postcard) can still be a nice way to let people know that you are thinking about them. In tourist areas, postcards are sold almost everywhere; sometimes *francobolli* (stamps) are also sold in the same shop as the postcards and souvenirs, but, in most cases, you must go to a *tabaccaio* (tobacco shop) to buy stamps. Once your postcard has been stamped, look for a *buca delle lettere* or *cassetta postale* (mailbox), a large red box which carries the sign *Poste* (Mail) over it. Some of these boxes have two slots, one that says *per la città* (for the city) and the other saying *per tutte le altre destinazioni* (for all other destinations). Just drop your mail to be sent in the appropriate slot.

Another way of mailing items abroad is to go directly to the *ufficio postale* (post office), which can be found in every town—even in the smallest. In small post offices, there will likely be just one *sportello*

171

(counter) to deal with all requests, while in larger post offices you must choose the correct counter. If you have items to mail, choose the *sportello pacchi* or *spedizioni* (parcels or mailing counter), which normally is clearly identified with a sign displaying an envelope. In very busy offices, you must take a number at the entrance and wait for your number to be called. Post offices are open Monday through Friday, from 8 A.M. to 1 P.M. in small towns, from 8 A.M. to 6 P.M. in cities.

Sa dirmi dov'è l'ufficio postale?
Sah DEER-mee doh-VEH loof-FEE-cho po-STAH-leh

Can you tell me where the post office is?

Scusi, qual è lo sportello spedizioni?
SCOO-zee quahl eh lo spor-TEL-lo speh-dee-tsee-OH-nee

Pardon me, which is the mail counter?

Scusi, devo prendere il numero?
SCOO-zee DEH-vo PREHN-deh-reh eel NOO-meh-ro

Pardon me, do I have to take a number?

Qual è l'orario di apertura dell'ufficio postale?
Quahl eh lo-RAH-ree-oh dee ah-pair-TOO-rah del-loo-FEE-cho po-STAH-leh

What are the opening hours of the post office?

 Vorrei spedire una lettera raccomandata in Canada. (*Vor-RAY speh-DEE-reh OO-nah LET-teh-rah rac-co-mahn-DAH-tah een CAH-nah-dah*): I'd like to send this letter to Canada via certified mail.

The standard way of delivery in Italy and abroad is the *posta prioritaria* (priority mail). If you are mailing important items, use the *posta racco-*

mandata (certified mail), which gives you proof of delivery and which you can track online on the Poste Italiane website (www.poste.it). Or you could use *posta assicurata* (insured mail), by which your letter or parcel is insured for a certain amount of money should it be lost. In these cases, you will be asked to *compilare un modulo* (fill out a form) with information regarding the sender and receiver.

Parcels can be sent using standard delivery service, called *pacco ordinario* (regular parcel), or by using a much faster method called *pacco celere internazionale* (international express courier). What it costs to mail parcels depends on the delivery service you choose, on the destination, and on the *peso* (weight). If you must send something but do not have a *scatola* (box), you can purchase one in every post office. In any case, if you have questions, tell the *addetto allo sportello* (counter employee) where your letter or parcel must go and he/she will help you get it there. If you have doubts and concerns, check the Poste Italiane website, which has an English link with all the information you may need.

Vorrei spedire questa lettera tramite posta assicurata. Cosa devo fare?	I'd like to mail this letter by insured mail. What do I need to do?

Vor-RAY speh-DEE-reh QUEH-stah
    LET-teh-rah trah-MEE-teh PO-stah
    as-see-coo-RAH-tah CO-sa
    DEH-vo FAH-reh

Devo spedire questo pacco negli USA. Qual è il metodo più rapido?

DEH-vo speh-DEE-reh QUEH-sto PAC-co NEL-yee oo-sah Quah-LEH eel MEH-toh-doh PEW RAH-pee-doh

I need to send this parcel to the USA. What is the fastest way?

Scusi, quanto costa spedire questo pacco in Canada?

SCOO-zee QUAHN-toh CO-stah speh-DEE-reh QUEH-sto PAC-co een CAH-nah-dah

Pardon me, how much is it to send this parcel to Canada?

Come si fa a fare il tracking della spedizione sul vostro sito?

CO-meh see fah ah FAH-reh eel tracking DEL-lah speh-dee-tsee-OH-neh sool VO-stro SEE-toh

How can I track the delivery on your website?

 Una carta telefonica per gli Stati Uniti, per favore.

(OO-nah CAHR-tah teh-leh-FO-nee-cah pair lyee STAH-tee Oo-NEE-tee pair fah-VO-reh): A phone card for the United States, please.

If you need to call your family at home in North America, the least expensive way is to use a *carta telefonica internazionale* (international phone card). Phone cards can easily be found at the *giornalaio* (newsstand), at the *tabaccaio* (tobacco shop), and in phone stores called *Punto 187*. Sometimes they are also sold at post offices or in some hotels, but it is uncommon.

There are many types of international phone cards—most are issued by Telecom, Italy's national phone company, and among those for the United States and Canada are those called No Distance, New Welcome, New Columbus, and Time. These cards have various *piani tariffari* (rate plans); so ask the shop assistant for advice. In general, however, they are *prepagate* (prepaid), usually cost between 5 and 10 euros, and allow you to call standard and mobile phones for different rates. Phone cards can be used from *telefoni pubblici* (public phones) and from some other phones, too, although not usually from hotel phones. In Italy there are public phones almost anywhere in the streets, in hotel lobbies, in department stores, and in shopping malls. Most public phones allow you to pay with a *carta di credito* (credit card), but that can be quite expensive, so it is best to purchase an international phone card first.

Come funziona questa scheda telefonica?
How does this phone card work?

CO-meh foon-TSEE-oh-nah
QUEH-stah SKEH-dah
teh-leh-FO-nee-cah

Vorrei una scheda per chiamare in Italia e all'estero.
I'd like a card to call in Italy and abroad.

Vor-RAY OO-nah SKEH-dah pair
kee-ah-MAH-reh een Ee-TAH-
lee-ah al-LEH-steh-ro

Qual è la scheda più conveniente per chiamare gli USA?
What is the cheapest phone card to call the USA?

Quah-LEH lah SKEH-dah PEW
cohn-veh-nee-EHN-teh pair
kee-ah-MAH-reh lyee oo-sah

Sa quanto costano le telefonate con questa scheda?	Do you know how much phone calls are with this card?
Sah QUAHN-toh CO-stah-no leh teh-leh-fo-NAH-teh kohn QUEH-stah SKEH-dah	

 Vorrei comprare un telefono cellulare. *(Vor-RAY cohm-PRAH-reh oon teh-LEH-fo-no chel-loo-LAH-reh):* I'd like to buy a mobile phone.

If you are staying in Italy for a long time or you do not want to rely on public phones for your calls, think of buying a *telefono cellulare* (mobile phone). Your American mobile phone can be used in Italy, too, but it can be prohibitively expensive. Buying a mobile phone in Italy may be a better solution.

Mobile phones are very popular in Italy, just like everywhere else, and you can easily find a store selling them. With mobile phones being so popular, good phones for a very fair price are readily available. If you are not looking for the trendiest or the most technologically sophisticated phone, you can buy a good phone for 50 euros or less. Moreover, you can buy a SIM *prepagata* or *ricaricabile* (prepaid SIM card), which can always be *ricaricata* (recharged) with the amount of money you prefer (usually fixed amounts between 10 and 250 euros). If you must recharge your SIM card, ask for a *ricarica telefonica per il cellulare* (mobile phone SIM recharge) at newsstands or tobacconists, specifying the amount of the recharge and your mobile phone provider. You can also recharge it online on your mobile phone provider website and pay with your credit card.

Even though buying a good phone is easy and quite inexpensive, finding the best rate for your needs can be difficult. In Italy there are four mobile phone providers: Tim, Vodafone, Wind, and 3, each with different rates and plans, so ask the shop assistant for help specifying your specific needs. When discussing the rate plan, ask about *tariffe SMS* (SMS costs), *segreteria telefonica* (voice mail), and *costi di attivazione e di chiusura* (activation and cancellation fees), which are not always so clear. Moreover, verify whether you are to pay for *chiamate ricevute dall'estero* (incoming calls from abroad).

Vorrei un telefono con una SIM ricaricabile.

Vor-RAY oon teh-LEH-fo-no kohn OO-nah esse-ee-emme ree-cah-ree-CAH-bee-leh

I'd like a mobile phone with a prepaid SIM.

Vorrei una ricarica da 50 euro.

Vor-RAY OO-nah ree-CAH-ree-cah dah cheen-QUAHN-tah eh-OO-ro

I'd like a SIM recharge for 50 euros.

Ho bisogno di chiamare all'estero. Qual è il piano tariffario migliore?

Oh bee-ZOHN-yo dee kee-ah-MAH-reh al-LES-teh-ro Quah-LEH eel pee-AH-no tah-reef-FAH-ree-oh meel-YO-reh

I need to call abroad. What is the best rate plan for me?

Vorrei una spiegazione sui vostri piani tariffari. Ad esempio, ci sono costi di attivazione e di chiusura?	I'd like an explanation regarding your rate plans. For example, are there activation and cancellation fees?

Vor-RAY OO-nah spee-eh-gah-tsee-OH-neh soo-EE VO-stree pee-AH-nee tah-reef-FAH-ree Ad eh-ZEHM-pee-oh chee SO-no CO-stee dee at-tee-vah-tsee-OH-neh eh dee kee-oo-ZOO-rah

 Potrei parlare con Michael Smith, per favore? *(Po-TRAY pahr-LAH-reh kohn Michael Smith pair fah-VO-reh):* May I speak with Michael Smith, please?

If you are on holiday in Italy, most of your phone calls will surely be to your family and friends back home. But you might also need to call someone in Italy, so it is useful to know a few phrases.

To call someone in Italy, you must dial the number preceded by the *prefisso locale* (local area code). For example, if you are calling someone in Rome, whose area code is 06, dial 06 followed by the phone number. It is mandatory to use the local area code for all calls within Italy, so Italians are used to specifying the code when they give out their phone number. You will also always find the local area codes given on business cards, in brochures, and in *guide telefoniche* (phone books). Italian phone books are divided into *pagine bianche* (white pages), where you can find all private numbers, and *pagine gialle* (yellow pages), where you can find all business listings. Phone directories are online as well, on www.paginebianche.it (for private numbers) and on www.paginegialle.it (for business listings).

To call a mobile within Italy, you do not need to worry about the specific code: The number you have been given or that you see on a business card is exactly the one to dial.

If you are calling Italy from abroad, first dial 011, then the country code, which is 39, then the local area code, and then the phone number; to call a mobile just dial 011-39 and then the mobile number. If you must call either Canada or the United States from Italy, dial the country code first, which is 001, and then the phone number, with area code if appropriate.

Qual è il Suo numero di telefono/ cellulare?
What is your phone/cell number?

Quah-LEH eel SOO-oh NOO-meh-ro
dee teh-LEH-fo-no/
chel-loo-LAH-reh

Ha una guida telefonica?
Do you have a phone directory?

Ah OO-nah goo-EE-dah
teh-leh-FO-nee-cah

Sa qual è il prefisso internazionale del Canada?
Do you know Canada's international country code?

Sah quah-LEH eel preh-FEES-so
een-tair-nah-tsee-oh-NAH-leh
del CAH-nah-dah

Scusi, ho sbagliato numero.
Sorry, I dialed the wrong number.

SCOO-zee oh sbahl-YAH-toh
NOO-meh-ro

C'è un Internet Point qui vicino? *(Cheh oon Internet Point kwee vee-CHEE-no):* Is there an Internet café near here?

The fastest, easiest, and cheapest way to keep in touch with friends and family back home is by using the Internet. If you do not want to bring your own laptop, you may use one at an Internet café or look for a place which has a PC for public use. Internet cafés are not so popular in Italy, but they can be found in large cities or in tourist areas, while it is more difficult to find one in smaller towns. Generally, all major bookstores like Mondadori, Feltrinelli, Rizzoli, Messaggerie Musicali, and Fnac have an Internet corner, but also look for public PCs in computer stores, bars, hotels, and other public places like airports and train stations. It is quite common to find Internet cafés near universities, and normally those Internet cafés offer other services such as *fotocopie* (photocopies), *stampe* (printing), *scansione digitale* (digital scanning), and *masterizzazione CD o DVD* (CD or DVD burning), which can be useful services, too. In cities, public libraries have an Internet corner, too. To find out where the nearest Internet point is, take a look at these two websites: http://cafe.ecs.net/ and www.cyber cafe.it, which give a full listing of Internet points in Italy. However, surfing the Net at an Internet café can be very expensive, in general from 3 to 5 euros per hour.

If you carry your own laptop with you, you can use it in most hotel rooms, but if you must have an Internet connection in your room, it is always better to double-check when making a reservation. Some public places may have a wireless connection, but this is still not very widespread in Italy. You might try looking for wireless in city libraries, bookstores, or very trendy cafés.

Quanto costa usare Internet per un'ora?	How much is it to use the Internet for an hour?
QUAHN-toh CO-stah oo-ZAH-reh EEN-tair-net pair oon-OH-rah	
C'è la connessione Internet nella stanza?	Does the room have an Internet connection?
Cheh lah kohn-nes-see-OH-neh EEN-tair-net NEL-lah STAHN-tsah	
Dove trovo una connessione wireless?	Where can I find a wireless connection?
DOH-veh TRO-vo OO-nah kohn-nes-see-OH-neh wireless	

 Vorrei una connessione Internet. Cosa devo fare? *(Vor-RAY OO-nah kohn-nes-see-OH-neh EEN-tair-net CO-zah DEH-vo FAH-reh):* I'd like to set up an Internet connection. What must I do?

If your plan is to stay in Italy for a long time and you are renting an apartment, you can have an Internet connection set up in the house. If the apartment already has a *linea telefonica* (phone line), the process is quite easy. Simply call an Internet provider and request *una connessione Internet* (an Internet connection); in most cases you can also do this online via each provider website. The main Internet providers in Italy are Telecom, Infostrada, Wind, Tiscali, and Tele2, each of them offering different connections at various rates. Usually the most convenient are those offering *accesso illimitato* (unlimited Internet access) for *a tariffa flat mensile* (monthly flat rate). With such a connection, you can use the Internet, chat, or call home with Skype for free.

If you really want to feel Italian and have an Italian e-mail address, set one up with www.libero.it, which is the most common e-mail provider in Italy.

Quanto costa la connessione flat?	How much is the flat-rate connection?
QUAHN-toh CO-stah lah kohn-nes-see-OH-neh flat	
Ci sono spese aggiuntive oppure è tutto incluso?	Are there additional costs or is everything included?
Chee SO-no SPEH-zeh ad-joon-TEE-veh op-POO-reh eh TOOT-toh een-CLOO-zo	
Fornite anche un indirizzo e-mail con la connessione?	Is an e-mail address included with the connection?
For-NEE-teh AHN-keh oon een-dee-REETS-so e-mail kohn lah kohn-nes-see-OH-neh	
Vorrei la connessione più veloce che avete.	I'd like the fastest connection you have.
Vor-RAY lah kohn-nes-see-OH-neh PEW veh-LO-cheh keh ah-VEH-teh	

 Sei su Facebook? *(Seh-ee soo Facebook):* Are you on Facebook?

In Italy, like in North America, the best way to keep in touch for the young generation is through Facebook. Also very popular programs are MySpace, YouTube, MSN, and Skype. Of course, e-mail is still a very strong tool for both the young and old generations.

Qual è la tua e-mail?

Quah-LEH lah too-ah e-mail

What is your e-mail address?

La mia e-mail è bello chiocciola libero punto it (bello@libero.it).

Lah MEE-ah e-mail eh BEH-loh kee-OH-chee-oh-lah POON-toh ee-tee

My e-mail bello at libero dot it (bello@libero.it).

Ci sentiamo su MSN.

Chee sehn-tee-AH-moh soo MSN

See you on MSN.

Chapter 18

Sports

 Chi gioca oggi? *(Kee JO-cah OD-jee):* Who's playing today?

Soccer is by far the most popular sport in Italy and is followed on a daily basis by the majority of Italians: men and women, children and seniors alike. Soccer players are highly regarded; their status is at the same level, if not higher, as Hollywood celebrities. When one asks *Chi gioca?*, by default, he/she is referring to that day's soccer game. Similarly, when one talks about *la nazionale* or the *Azzurri*, he/she is talking about the national soccer team.

Italians are very proud of their favorite club team and their national team. The *Azzurri* national team is among the very best in the world and has won the World Cup (*Coppa del Mondo*) on four different occasions: 1934, 1938, 1982, and 2006. Only Brazil has a better record.

Other very popular sports in Italy are *Formula Uno, pallacanestro* or *basket, ciclismo, pallavolo,* and *boxe* (boxing). Baseball and *football americano* (to distinguish it from soccer/*football*) are not popular sports in Italy.

Contro chi gioca la nazionale?
KOHN-tro kee JO-cah lah nah-tsee-oh-NAH-leh

Against which team is the national team playing?

Chi è stato convocato?
Kee eh STAH-toh kohn-vo-CAH-toh

Which players were selected (to be part of the national team)?

Quando è la partita di ritorno?
QUAHN-doh eh lah pahr-TEE-tah dee ree-TOR-no

When is the second-leg match?

In quale stadio stanno giocando?
Een QUAH-leh STAH-dee-oh STAN-no jo-CAHN-doh

In which stadium are they playing?

 Secondo te, chi vincerà lo scudetto/il campionato? *(SEH-kohn-doh teh kee veen-cheh-RAH lo scoo-DET-toh/eel cahm-pee-oh-NAH-toh):* In your opinion, who will win the *scudetto* (championship shield)/(soccer) championship?

On Saturday and Sunday, Italians religiously follow the *campionato* with their many different leagues. The first soccer tournament dates to 1898. The *Serie A* (Premiere League), the most important league, is the source of discussions, speculations, and debates, from August through the end of May. These lively discussions take place among family members, friends, and colleagues, but also in newspapers and on radio and television shows. The discussion becomes even more intense with the European Champions League games (*Coppa dei Campioni* [Champion's league]), usually played during midweek. Even during the summer, when the soccer championship is resting, Italians are discussing the *calcio-mercato*, that is, the many trades between clubs to acquire the best players.

Since 1946, Italians have been legally betting on soccer games with *Totocalcio* (soccer pool) and its famous *schedina* (betting pool), which is run by CONI, the Italian Olympic Committee, and whose profit is used to promote all sports in Italy. The idea behind the *schedina* is simple: One must guess the results of thirteen (now fourteen) soccer games, by using a 1 to indicate a win for the home team, a 2 for a win for the away team, and an X for a tie. For fifty years the *schedina* was the lottery game par excellence in Italy and it was part of a national tradition. Its symbols 1, X, 2 were part of everyday language; the number 13 became the Italian lucky number as guessing all thirteen results would make you a millionaire. In the past ten years, however, the game is somewhat in decline because of the competition of many lottery games with higher jackpots.

Hai giocato la schedina?
Aye jo-CAH-toh lah skeh-DEE-nah

Did you play the *schedina*?

Per quale squadra fai il tifo?
Pair QUAH-leh SQUAH-drah fye
    eel TEE-fo

Which is your favorite team?

Chi sono le favorite?
Kee SO-no leh fah-vo-REE-teh

Which are the favorite teams (to win the championship)?

Qual è il tuo pronostico per la partita di oggi?
Quah-LEH eel TOO-oh pro-NO-stee-co
    pair lah pahr-TEE-tah dee OD-jee

What's your prediction for today's game?

Che partita fanno vedere in televisione? *(Keh pahr-TEE-tah FAN-no veh-DEH-reh een teh-leh-vee-zee-OH-neh):* Which game are they showing on television?

The cost for a ticket (*un biglietto*) to watch a soccer match at the *stadio* (stadium) varies from as low as 30 euros to over 100 euros for the best seats. You will find that online tickets are exorbitantly higher. If you are a soccer fan and cannot afford or find a ticket, there are plenty of opportunities to watch a game on television or even listen to it on the radio. On the RAIRadio1 program *Tutto il calcio minuto per minuto*, which has been running since 1960, you can listen to all *Serie A* games and enjoy the live and exciting play-by-play action by some of the best radio announcers in the world. Many television networks also dedicate a large part of their Saturday and Sunday programs to soccer games and to programs almost completely dedicated to soccer, showing the goals and the highlights of all games, assigning a score to each individual player, the coaches, and the referees. Very common is the so-called *moviola*, a frame-by-frame replay used in television programs (but not in the field) to analyze the decisions of the referee (*arbitro*) regarding penalty kicks (*i rigori*), goals *(le reti, i goals)*, whether a player was offside (*fuori gioco, offside*) or not, etc.

If you enter a room or a sports bar where a game is being shown on television, use the questions below to get instant updates. Just make sure to ask these questions at a time when the action is not too intense!

Qual è il risultato? / Quanto stanno?
What's the score?
Quah-LEH eel ree-zool-TAH-toh / KWAHN-toh STAHN-no

Chi vince/sta vincendo/ha vinto?
Kee VEEN-cheh/stah veen-
   CHEHN-doh/ah VEEN-toh

Who is winning/is winning/won?

Chi gioca in porta?
Kee JO-cah een POR-tah

Who is playing in the goal?

Chi ha segnato?
Kee ah sehn-YAH-toh

Who scored?

 Chi è l'arbitro? *(Kee eh LAHR-bee-tro)*: Who is the referee?

In Italy, as the expression goes, there are 50 million coaches. Every Italian believes that he or she has the knowledge to be a soccer coach (*allenatore*). For this reason, before each game Italians feel entitled to propose *la formazione della squadra* (the team lineup) for that game; during the game they like to comment on what they watch; afterward they analyze the game. If you are an avid soccer fan and would like to comment on the game you are watching or listening to, you will have ample opportunities to do so. However, do not make your comments during a very critical or intense time in the game; furthermore, make sure that your comments do not upset the majority of people present.

Ma perché non fa giocare Del Piero?
Mah pair-KEH nohn fah jo-CAH-reh Del Pee-EH-ro

But why does he (the coach) not let Del Piero play?

Il tackle meritava un cartellino giallo.
Eel TAK-kel meh-ree-TAH-vah oon cahr-tel-LEE-no JAL-lo

The tackle deserved a yellow card.

Il giocatore meritava l'espulsione; era un fallo da cartellino rosso.

Eel jo-cah-TOH-reh meh-ree-TAH-vah leh-spool-zee-OH-neh; EH-rah oon FAL-lo dah cahr-tel-LEE-no ROS-so

The player deserved to be expelled from the game; the foul deserved a red card.

Ma l'arbitro e i segnalinee cosa fanno, dormono? È rigore... altro che punizione.

Mah LAHR-bee-tro eh ee sehn-ya-lee-NEH-eh COH-sah FAN-no DOR-mo-no Eh ree-GO-reh AHL-tro keh poo-nee-tsee-OH-neh

But what are the referee and the linesmen doing, sleeping? It was a penalty kick not a free kick!

 Chi è prima in classifica? *(Kee eh PREE-mah een clas-SEE-fee-cah):* Who is first in the standings?

For Italians, meeting friends to discuss soccer results on Sunday evening or Monday morning is a way to socialize and to get informed if someone missed the live action. If you missed a game and want an instant update, you might want to visit the local sports bar, enjoy the lively discussion, and participate in the conversation. Soccer, like many other sports, is a way to break all sorts of barriers. Sports fans will definitely answer all your questions.

Qual è stato il risultato di Milan-Roma?

Quah-LEH eh STAH-toh eel ree-zool-TAH-toh dee Mee-LAHN-RO-mah

What was the score for AC Milan-Rome?

Ha vinto la Juventus?	Did Juventus win?
Ah VEEN-toh lah Yoo-VEHN-toos	
Chi è il capocannoriere?	Who is the leading scorer?
Kee eh eel cah-po-can-no-ree-EH-reh	
Chi ha segnato per l'Inter?	Who scored for Inter Milan?
Kee ah sehn-YA-toh pair LEEN-tair	

 Chi c'é nel girone dell'Inter? *(Kee cheh nel jee-RO-neh del-LEEN-tair):* Who is in the round-robin together with Inter Milan?

Besides Italian championship and national team games, Italians closely follow the European Champion's League tournament, a tournament in which the best European teams, the winners of the national championship, and the second- to fourth-placed teams participate. Italian teams have the best record in this championship; Italy has won eleven times and has been runner-up fourteen times.

Another very prestigious tournament (*torneo*) is the UEFA Cup. The participants in this tournament are the National Cup winners and the three teams that placed immediately after the Champions League team. The winner of the Champions League plays against the winner of the UEFA Cup for the *Supercoppa* (Europe Super Cup). Following a similar format, the winner of the Italian Championship winner plays the *Copia Italia* winner for an Italian *Supercoppa*.

The most prestigious European cup is the UEFA European Championship, which Italy won only once in 1968.

These tournaments are divided into several stages: in the *turno preliminare* (preliminary/qualifying round), teams are divided into *gironi* (round-robin groups); the winners and second-place teams advance to the *quarti di finali* (quarterfinals) then to the *semifinali* (semifinals) and the *finali* (finals) by playing two direct elimination games, one at home (*in casa*) and one away from home (*fuori casa*). The finals consist of one game only.

The *Pallone d'oro* (*Golden Ball*) is the most prestigious award for individual players. It is awarded annually by European journalists to the single top player in any European league.

Chi gioca in casa?	Which team is playing at home?
Kee JO-cah een CAH-zah	
Siamo solo al turno preliminare!	We are only in the preliminary round!
See-AH-mo SO-lo ahl TOOR-no preh-lee-mee-NAH-reh	
Chi si è qualificato per le semifinali?	Which teams qualified for the semifinals?
Kee see eh quah-lee-fee-CAH-toh pair leh seh-mee-fee-NAH-lee	
Quando si giocano le finali?	When are the finals played?
QUAHN-doh see JO-cah-no leh fee-NAH-lee	

 Chi ha comprato il Milan? (*Kee ah cohm-PRAH-toh eel Mee-LAHN*)*:* Whom (which players) did AC Milan buy?

Even during the summer, when the Italian championship is not being played, Italian fans (*tifosi*) still have much to discuss. In fact, it is during this period that Italian teams trade players. Fans follow the *calcio-mercato* news and have solid opinions about the players that are needed to improve each team. Some will suggest that their *squadra* (team) needs a better *portiere* (goalkeeper) or defense (*difesa*); others will prefer that their team strengthen the *centrocampo* (midfield) or the attack (*attacco*). The *allenatore* (coach/trainer) is often the scapegoat for a poor season. It seems each fan can come up with a solution to better the team with his/her own possible *formazione* (lineup).

Many fans will watch the team during their *allenamento* (practice) or during the *partite amichevoli* (friendly/preseason games).

Alla Roma serve un centrocampista forte. AL-lah RO-mah SAIR-veh oon chehn-tro-cahm-PEE-stah FOR-teh	Roma needs a strong midfielder.
Quando va in ritiro il Napoli? QUAHN-doh vah een ree-TEE-ro eel NAH-po-lee	When does Naples start its training camp?
È solo una partita amichevole? Eh SO-lo OO-nah pahr-TEE-tah ah-mee-KEH-vo-leh	Is it only a preseason/friendly game?
Chi gioca in difesa? Kee JO-cah een dee-FEH-zah	Who is playing defense?

 Chi ha vinto la tappa? *(Kee ah VEEN-toh lah TAP-pah):* Who won the cycling stage?

Ciclismo (cycling) is another very popular sport in Italy, with thousands of riders cycling every day. The *Giro d'Italia*, the most popular cycling race in Italy, is 100 years old; it is divided into stages which total about 2500 kilometers covering almost all regions of Italy, and it lasts almost the entire month of May. Each stage has a winner; the overall leader wears the *maglia rosa* (pink jersey), but there are many colored jerseys for a variety of leaders. For example, the green jersey is assigned to the leading mountain climbers. Cyclists (*ciclisti*) are unofficially divided into three categories; there are sprinters, *scalatori* (mountain climbers), and *gregari* (support cyclists who work for the *capitano* [team captain]).

Chi ha vinto la tappa a cronometro?	Who won the cronometer stage?
Kee ah VEEN-toh lah TAP-pah ah cro-no-MEH-tro	
Di quanti chilometri è la tappa?	How many kilometers is the stage?
Dee QUAHN-tee kee-LO-meh-tree eh lah TAP-pah	
A che ora è previsto l'arrivo?	At what time is the arrival expected?
Ah keh OH-rah eh preh-VEE-sto lar-REE-vo	
Chi è la maglia rosa?	Who is the overall leader?
Kee eh lah MAHL-yah RO-zah	

 Dov'è il prossimo Gran Premio? *(Doh-VEH eel PROS-see-mo Grahn PREH-mee-oh)*: Where is the next Grand Prix?

The Ferrari, or simply *La Rossa*, with its fifteen *Formula Uno* (Formula One) titles since its beginning in 1952, is perhaps the most celebrated car in the world and is a symbol of elegance, power, and speed. *Formula Uno* races are followed by sports fans of every nationality and Italian fans are no exception. Alfa Romeo and Maserati are also cars that have fared well in car racing. There are two Formula One titles: The most prestigious is for drivers (*piloti*); the other is for *costruttori* (constructors). Before each Grand Prix, there are the trials (*le prove*) which will decide the starting order for the actual race. The car which cleared the shortest time for a lap will be assigned the *pole position*. During the race (*la gara*), cars will stop to change the tires (*le ruote*) and for fuel.

Chi guida la classifica dei piloti? Kee goo-EE-dah lah clas-SEE-fee- cah day pee-LO-tee	Who is leading the driver standings?
Chi guida la classifica dei costruttori? Kee goo-EE-dah lah clas-SEE-fee-cah day co-stroot-TOH-ree	Who is leading the constructor standings?
Chi è in pole position? Kee eh een pole position	Who has pole position?
A che posto si trova la Ferrari? Ah keh PO-sto see TRO-vah lah Fer-RAH-ree	What place is the Ferrari in?

 Quando incomincia il campionato del mondo di sci?
*(QUAHN-doh een-co-MEEN-cha eel cahm-pee-oh-NAH-toh del
MOHN-doh dee she):* When does the skiing world championship
start?

Very popular sports in Italy also include *pallacanestro* or *basket*, *tennis*, *boxe*, *atletica leggera* (track and field), *pallavolo* (volleyball), *pallanuoto* (water polo), *motociclismo* (motorcycling), *sci* (ski), *ginnastica* (gymnastics), *nuoto* (swimming), and *scherma* (fencing). Many are the international and Olympics (*Olimpiadi*) successes of Italian teams and athletes in these disciplines.

Less popular sports are *rugby*, *baseball*, *cricket*, *football americano* (football), *pallamano* (handball), and *hockey*.

Chi ha vinto nello stile libero? Kee ah VEEN-toh NEL-lo STEE-leh LEE-beh-ro	Who won the (swimming) free-style race?

Quando si disputa lo slalom gigante?

QUAHN-doh see dee-SPOO-tah lo SLAH-lohm jee-GAHN-teh

When is the giant slalom race?

Quanti punti ha fatto Andrea Bargnani nella gara contro i Knicks?

QUAHN-tee POON-tee ah FAT-toh Ahn-DREH-ah Bahrn-YA-nee NEL-lah GAH-rah KOHN-tro ee Knicks

How many points did Andrea Bargnani score against the Knicks?

Chi ha vinto il torneo internazionale di tennis a Roma?

Kee ah VEEN-toh eel tor-NEH-oh een-tair-nah-tsee-oh-NAH-leh dee TEN-nees ah RO-mah

Who won the Rome Masters Tournament?

 Hai comprato La Gazzetta dello Sport? *(Aye kohm-PRAH-toh Lah gahts-SET-tah DEL-lo sport):* Did you buy the *Gazzetta dello Sport*?

Italy is one of the few nations that has not one but three daily newspapers exclusively dedicated to sports: *La Gazzetta dello Sport*, *Il Corriere dello Sport*, and *Tuttosport*. All three newspapers have a long tradition: the *Gazzetta* dates to 1896, the *Corriere* to 1924, *Tuttosport* to 1945. All three newspapers also have a wide national circulation: the *Gazzetta* has a circulation of over 500,000 copies; in 1982, when Italy won the World Cup, the *Gazzetta* sold almost 3 million copies and the *Corriere* almost 2 million.

There are also many weekly and monthly sports magazines, many of them specializing in a specific sport.

Please remember that Italian daily, weekly, and monthly newspapers, as well as magazines, are sold at specialized newspaper stands (*edicola*), at smoke shops (*tabacchino*), and at local bars.

Similarly, there are many cable television and pay-TV programs dedicated exclusively to sports. These give you the opportunity to watch not only various sports events but also many sports talk shows.

Hai visto l'incontro di basket alla televisione?

Aye VEE-sto leen-KOHN-tro dee BAHS-ket AL-lah teh-leh-vee-zee-OH-neh

Did you watch the basketball game on television?

Quale trasmissione televisiva ti piace di più: 90° minuto oppure La giostra del gol?

QUAH-leh trahz-mees-see-OH-neh teh-leh-vee-ZEE-vah tee pee-AH-cheh dee PEW: No-vahn-TEH-zee-mo mee-NOO-toh op-POO-reh Lah JO-strah del gol

Which television program do you like best: *90° minuto* or *La giostra del gol*?

Pensi che Beckham rimarrà con il Milan?

PEHN-zee keh Beckham ree-mahr-RAH kohn eel Mee-LAHN

Do you think that Beckham will remain with AC Milan?

Che voto hanno dato nella pagella a Ronaldinho?

Keh VO-toh AHN-no DAH-toh NEL-lah pah-JEL-lah ah Ro-nahl-DEEN-yoh

What mark did Ronaldinho get in his (game) report card?

Andiamo a fare un po' di jogging. *(Ahn-dee-AH-mo ah FAH-reh oon poh dee jogging):* Let's go jogging.

As previously discussed, Italians like to read about sports and watch it on television. Their involvement in personal sports activities is, however, somewhat limited. Many go to the *palestra* (gym), the *centri benessere* (wellness centers), or the *centri sportivi* (sports centers), but in general Italians do not attend as avidly as North Americans. The cost of a gym membership is about 20 to 30 euros per month. Italians stay *in forma* (in shape) by doing a lot of walking and other natural activities; also, they use bicycles much more than North Americans.

In schools, two hours a week are dedicated to gym activities. However, school-related sports tournaments are not nearly as common as in North America. Outside school, the most popular sports activities for Italian children are soccer, basketball, volleyball, bicycling, dance, aqua fitness, swimming, and yoga.

Dove trovo una piscina all'aperto? DO-veh TROH-vo OO-nah pee-SHE-nah al-lah-PAIR-toh	Where can I find an outdoor pool?
Quanto costa un abbonamento per la palestra? QUAHN-toh CO-stah oon ab-bo-nah-MEHN-toh pair lah pah-LEH-strah	How much is a gym membership?
Vi sono dei campi da tennis disponibili? Vee SO-no day CAHM-pee dah TEN-nees dee-spo-NEE-bee-lee	Are there any tennis courts available?
Vorrei fare un po' di sollevamento pesi. Vor-RAY FAH-reh oon po dee sol-leh-vah-MEHN-toh PEH-zee	I would like to do some weight lifting.

Forza Italia! *(FORT-sah Ee-TAH-lee-ah)*: Go, Italy, go!

Sports fans all over the world support their team by going to games. Their support is often shown by cheering their team (or booing the opposite team) during the game or by displaying large support banners. Holding support banners in Italy is quite common and well coordinated in the stadiums; slogans used by fans are often collected in books as if it were an art form. While the Italian national soccer team is playing, the fans will encourage the players with *Forza Italia!* or *Forza Azzurri!* while proudly waving the Italian flag.

Italia! Italia! Italia!
Ee-TAH-lee-ah Ee-TAH-lee-ah
    Ee-TAH-lee-ah

Go, Italy, go!

Forza Milan!
FORT-sah Mee-LAHN

Go, Milan, go!

Forza Roma! Forza lupi!
FORT-sah RO-mah FORT-sah
    LOO-pee

Go, Rome, go! Go, Rome, go! (*lupo* = wolf; the reference is to the symbol of AC Roma)

Viva la Juve! Abbasso l'Inter!
VEE-vah lah YOO-veh Ab-BAS-so
    LEEN-tair

Go, Juve, go! Down with Inter!

The Right Phrase for Every Situation...Every Time.

3/2010

Perfect Phrases for Building Strong Teams
Perfect Phrases for Business Letters
Perfect Phrases for Business Proposals and Business Plans
Perfect Phrases for Business School Acceptance
Perfect Phrases for College Application Essays
Perfect Phrases for Cover Letters
Perfect Phrases for Customer Service
Perfect Phrases for Dealing with Difficult People
Perfect Phrases for Dealing with Difficult Situations at Work
Perfect Phrases for Documenting Employee Performance Problems
Perfect Phrases for Executive Presentations
Perfect Phrases for Landlords and Property Managers
Perfect Phrases for Law School Acceptance
Perfect Phrases for Lead Generation
Perfect Phrases for Managers and Supervisors
Perfect Phrases for Managing Your Small Business
Perfect Phrases for Medical School Acceptance
Perfect Phrases for Meetings
Perfect Phrases for Motivating and Rewarding Employees
Perfect Phrases for Negotiating Salary & Job Offers
Perfect Phrases for Perfect Hiring
Perfect Phrases for the Perfect Interview
Perfect Phrases for Performance Reviews
Perfect Phrases for Real Estate Agents & Brokers
Perfect Phrases for Resumes
Perfect Phrases for Sales and Marketing Copy
Perfect Phrases for the Sales Call
Perfect Phrases for Setting Performance Goals
Perfect Phrases for Small Business Owners
Perfect Phrases for the TOEFL Speaking and Writing Sections
Perfect Phrases for Writing Grant Proposals
Perfect Phrases in American Sign Language for Beginners
Perfect Phrases in French for Confident Travel
Perfect Phrases in German for Confident Travel
Perfect Phrases in Italian for Confident Travel
Perfect Phrases in Spanish for Confident Travel to Mexico
Perfect Phrases in Spanish for Construction
Perfect Phrases in Spanish for Gardening and Landscaping
Perfect Phrases in Spanish for Household Maintenance and Childcare
Perfect Phrases in Spanish for Restaurant and Hotel Industries

Visit mhprofessional.com/perfectphrases for a complete product listing.

Learn more. Do more.